WHITE MOKO
TIM TIPENE
stories from my life

OneTree HOUSE

Produced with the assistance of

To my parents and family
This is where the cycles of abuse and violence,
that have hindered us for so long, stops.

First published by OneTree House Ltd, New Zealand

Text © Tim Tipene, 2020
9780995106789

Some names and identifying details have been changed to protect the privacy of individuals and the actions described are as the author remembers them.

All rights reserved. No part of this publication may be reproduced, stored in a retrieval system or transmitted in any form or by any means, electronic, mechanical, photocopying, recording or otherwise, without the prior permission of the publisher.

Cover design: dahlDESIGN
Printed in New Zealand: Wickliffe, a division of Blue Star Group (NZ) Limited

10 9 8 7 6 5 4 3 2 1   0 1 2 3 / 2

CHAPTERS

White fella	5	The art of self-sabotage	148
My Timmy me	11	Mt Eden Prison	154
Singled out	19	Monster	160
Home was a scary place	25	Katie	167
A hunk of wood	30	Facing Dad	169
Goodbye to the whānau	35	Wanting to be different	175
The perceptions of others	46	Tipene	180
Dreaming for kidnap	54	The Wooden Fish	183
Successes	59	Affluently high	189
Herbie and Princess	64	Moko Mā	194
Omaha	71	Kura Toa	200
Getting to do karate	75	The swordsman	210
Heta and Mary	81	Shaun	216
Running away	88	A love story - part one	220
Kenji	94	Here comes the sun	225
High school	99	Beijing watermelon	227
The magic room	104	Daddy's girl	233
Crazy ninja	114	A good father	237
Scissors	120	A love story - part two	240
Fish and chips on the beach	126	Life is good	243
Contradicting influences	132	To the reader	247
Choice	138	Photographs	248
Mt Tabor	143		

WHITE FELLA

'Who are you?'

'Where do you come from?'

'How did you get the name Tipene? You're a white fella.'

These are questions that I have constantly been asked throughout my life. Everywhere I've gone I've had to explain who I am, to Māori and Pākehā alike.

Some haven't been polite about it either.

One afternoon after I had finished running my community Warrior Kids class for children at the Henderson Rec Centre, a Māori woman approached me. She was a resource teacher of learning and behaviour, and at only 27 I could see that she was a lot older than me. She held up one of my Warrior Kids brochures and it was obvious she wasn't happy.

'Tipene,' she read aloud from the bio on the back.

'Yes,' I replied.

'That's a Māori name,' she said, looking me up and down.

Flustered, I shuffled my feet. I knew what was coming next.

'You don't look Māori to me!' the woman snapped. 'Where's the Māori in you?'

'You mean colour?' I asked.

'Yeah, why is a Pākehā pretending to be Māori?' she growled. 'Is it just to get funding?'

'I don't go for funding,' I replied.

Disgruntled, she soon left, and I fell into the usual pit of despair and rejection that I always felt following such encounters.

When I told my Uncle Blake about the incident, he said I should have shown the woman a brown spot on the back of my ear. My whānau have always been quick with cheeky comebacks.

It wasn't just Māori challenging my use of the name Tipene though. Many white women took offence to it too.

I was once asked to speak as an author at a library on the North Shore in Auckland. While I sat in the tearoom waiting to present, a librarian came in to have her break.

The woman told me she had only recently moved to New Zealand from England. She chatted with me about why I was at the library and about the books I had written. She was pleasant to begin with, but then her demeanour changed.

'Where did you get the name Tipene from?' she asked. 'Did you think that by using a Māori name you would sell more books?'

Before I could even answer, the woman went into a rant about how disrespectful it was for me, a white man, to be using a Māori name. She told me I had no right to use the name Tipene. That it was cultural misappropriation. That it was insulting to Māori and I should go back to my original name. She demanded to know where I had gotten the name from as though she were an authority on the matter.

I thought of Uncle Blake, and considered telling the woman I had found the name in a box of cereal, but then figured it probably wasn't worth the argument. Instead I told her about the origins of my name. She wasn't convinced.

Whenever anyone challenged me about my name I would recite my family history to them. After years of explaining myself I have it down pat.

I am a Tipene. My full last name is Waitai-Tipene. I became a Tipene at the age of two when the whānau took me in as their own, and I was brought up as such. My birth mother married into the whānau and I was legally adopted by them. My notice of adoption and birth certificate both state that I am a Tipene.

My grandfather's name was William (Tim) Waitai-Tipene and I am regarded as his namesake.

In Ngāti Whātua my mountain is called Tokatoka, my river, Wairoa.

My Ngāti Whātua marae are Rīpia and Naumai.

In Ngāti Kurī my mountain is Maunga Piko, Parengarenga is the sea.

My Ngāti Kurī marae is Te Hiku o te Ika.

My great-grandparents on my grandfather's side are Hetaraka Waitai-Tipene and Miria Waru. My grandmother was Dorothy (Dolly) Tahu, and her parents were Waaka Taimona Tahu and Eva Angell.

I don't know for sure why my family only used Tipene for a last name instead of Waitai-Tipene; however I do remember discussions in the whānau about the ruling Pākehā being accustomed to short names and that we had to assimilate. Later in her life my grandmother went to court and fought for the right to return to Waitai-Tipene. She won; however my Dad kept us as Tipene.

¤ ¤ ¤

When I was a child everything seemed simple, but my identity became complicated in my teens. There was strong division at my high school and in the community – two camps. You were either Māori or you were Pākehā. There was no in-between. Each day I looked in the mirror, trying to work out who I was. I saw white, yet I identified as Māori.

A Māori girl in my class complained about me to a Māori teacher, so the teacher took it upon herself to give me an extra lesson.

'You're not Māori!' she said. 'Your dad might be Māori, but you're not.'

The girl got in on the lecture.

'See,' she said. 'I told you, Tim. Just because your last name is Māori doesn't mean that you are. So stop hanging out with Māori kids. Go and be white like you're supposed to be.'

When mates asked me to join the kapa haka group at school I thought it best not to. While I hung out with my Māori mates after school, during school hours I stayed away from them, and hung out with only my white mates instead. Even though I had been brought up Māori, I didn't want to be seen as a white kid who was trying to be Māori.

My mate Cyril wasn't happy about that.

'Why aren't you hanging out with us anymore?' he asked.

I didn't know what to say.

Other friends of mine wouldn't accept it. They kept calling me a White Māori.

'Why are you trying to be a Pākehā?' Rueben said. 'You're not Pākehā. You're one of us—you're just white.'

Funnily enough that same teacher at high school, who told me that I wasn't Māori, would acknowledge me just a few years later. She encouraged me in my work and helped me to name my school for Warrior Kids.

'Kura Toa,' she said. 'That's the name. Now you go out and teach our people, boy.'

That was the weird thing—there were so many mixed messages. One moment I was being acknowledged as Māori, the next as Pākehā. And while people were making out there were benefits to having a Māori name, that wasn't my experience. People treated me differently as soon as they knew I was a Tipene, and not in a good way. My siblings and I were known as the 'Tippanee Kids', and that followed us right through school.

When I was a young man trying to get a job employers were quick to respond to my surname. I phoned up about a job vacancy at a petrol station in Helensville. The interview on the phone went great. It seemed that I had the job in the bag, until the man asked me for my last name. I had come to dread this question when inquiring about jobs and the reactions that followed.

'Tipene,' I said.

'That's a Māori name, isn't it?' he queried.

I braced for impact. 'Yes,' I said.

'We don't hire your kind here,' the man replied, hanging up.

¤ ¤ ¤

Nana, Poppa and my many aunties and uncles were all proud of me, their blonde-haired, blue-eyed white moko.

As an adult, though, I ended up apologising to many Māori for having the name Tipene, since so many were upset by it. Speakers on some marae were keen to address the matter in front of everyone. During their speech they would tell me that I should stop using a Māori name and go back to a Pākehā name.

But I couldn't do that. That would be trampling on the mana of Poppa and Nana and the whānau who had raised me and given me the name. Imagine the insult. It would be spitting in their faces.

When my Aunty Martha Hetaraka was gravely sick I went up north to console her, but after she told me that this would be the last time I would see her alive she ended up having to console me. While her body was failing, Aunty's mind was as sharp as it had always been.

'You've been good to this family, Timmy,' she said, giving me her blessing.

My whānau lay claim to me, they accept me. I know who I am and where I come from. My name is Tim Waitai-Tipene and I don't apologise for it anymore. Becoming a Tipene was my path in life and I am proud of it.

Growing up these experiences were difficult, and I took them all personally, especially since I was also facing rejection from my parents in my own home. Now looking back, though, I can see that the reaction of others was simply just that. Their reaction. It had nothing to do with me. It was a sign of the times. The 70s, 80s and 90s. There was a lot of racism and prejudice towards Māori then. There was talk of percentages and how much Māori blood people had. Māori were reclaiming their identity, their language and culture. Government funding was being made available for Māori in a number of areas such as education, health and social services, and there were Pākehā who took advantage of that. They saw Māori and their culture as a commodity. Pākehā organisations would associate themselves with Māori in order to access funding. Sadly, it still happens today.

While I took the projections of others on board, those people knew nothing of my childhood and my whānau. Considering the lack of confidence and security in myself I had at the time, I can understand why I took the hurt on, yet it was never mine to carry.

I have thought that a mataora (ta moko of the face), might be the answer.

It would be an extension of me and an acknowledgement of my heritage.

'It's your right to get ta moko on your face,' my Aunty Mabel Waru said when I discussed it with her. 'But I'll be in the ground before I let you do that to your face,' she added. 'You don't need it, Timmy. You know who you are, you know your whakapapa.'

William Tim Waitai-Tipene

Dorothy (Dolly) Tahu

Aunty Mabel Waru, Aunty Babe Parata Tim and Aunty Joy Anderson.

Tim with the cousins

MY TIMMY ME

Nana and Poppa Tipene lived on Swanson Road in West Auckland, just in front of the Waitematā Rugby Club. One of my earliest memories is being in a large makeshift tent that stood off the side of the house. It was when Poppa died.

The tangihanga was held at the home. Cars were parked everywhere and the tent was jam-packed full of people. It was 1976, I was four years old and sitting on a mattress next to Poppa's open coffin with Nana and other women. Aunties seated on the other side of the coffin called for me with open arms, so naturally I went to crawl over Poppa to get to them. The women gasped and I was pulled off Poppa and made to go around the coffin. I couldn't understand this at the time because I had always climbed on Poppa when he was alive.

Poppa was buried up on the hill at Waikumete Cemetery. He was considered a chiefly person, and it's said that I take after him. (No pressure there then.)

Mum's dad died around the same time. I called him poppa too, yet I didn't know him all that well. I didn't have the closeness with him that I'd had with Poppa Tipene. I remember my older brother Shaun getting to see Mum's dad when he was sick, but I was kept away.

I felt bad at his funeral, though, when I was encouraged to throw dirt down on his coffin. I would never have thrown dirt at him when he was alive. He was buried at Waikumete Cemetery too, down in the valley. I remembered it so well that I was able to find his grave again as an adult. Now that both of my poppas were gone I no longer had a grandfather.

¤ ¤ ¤

At Nana's house it was often boil-ups of pūhā and brisket for dinner. Sometimes there was fry bread. I liked it when the bread was still warm, smothered with butter and jam. Nana would sit at the kitchen table drinking tea and smoking cigarette after cigarette. Although I never took up the habit of smoking I have always enjoyed the smell of tobacco because it reminds me of my grandmother.

With Poppa gone it was only Nana and my four uncles with special needs living at the house on Swanson Road—Uncle Athol, Uncle Ray, Uncle Tom (also known as Tomcat), and Uncle Harry. Some times Uncle Mike Waru would stay to help Nana out.

Uncle Harry was the eldest of the four brothers still at home. He was also the tallest and strongest. He liked to mix warm tea in a big bowl and break large quantities of Weet-Bixes or Huntley and Palmers crackers into it with his spoon. He would eat that any time of the day. Uncle Harry didn't talk—he grunted. He mostly stayed in his bedroom with the door partly closed, and Nana said that no one was allowed to go in there. It became a thing where older cousins liked to dare younger ones to enter Uncle Harry's room. Any children who did venture in were met with a barrage of incoherent yells from Uncle. The kids would come tearing out of the room, full of fear, and many have never forgotten it till this day.

As fearful as it was, I just wanted to talk to Uncle Harry, and in doing so I found that he didn't yell at me so much.

Uncle Athol used to walk up to the shops to get bread, milk and cigarettes. Uncle Ray was also known as Dearie, and he would stay close to Nana. Uncle Tom joked around and liked to hang out at the rugby club.

Those four uncles were the best. Uncles Athol, Ray and Tom were always so loving and engaging with us young ones, and they always kept us safe.

¤ ¤ ¤

Whānau were constantly dropping in to Nana's. Uncle Athol would make a pot of tea, and white bread would be put on the table with butter and jam. Sometimes the whānau brought cake. I had a lot of cousins, and when we weren't at the Waitematā Rugby Club watching my dad, other uncles and cousins play rugby we would be playing out back in the yard or lying on the floor in the lounge watching television. Nana would lie on the couch watching too. If us kids got too noisy Nana would tell Uncle Athol to bring her the hose.

'Now if you bloody kids don't shut up you're gonna get it!' Nana would say, holding up the short length of rubber hose.

Nana never hit me. I know my uncles copped it though.

Some evenings I got to watch TV with Nana in her bedroom. That was a special treat because few got to go into Nana's room.

Mum was in the habit of dropping me off all over the place when I was a child. Sometimes I was left with complete strangers, sometimes left to play at a park. It turned out I was Mum's cover story. She was telling people she was doing something with me when in actual fact she was off doing other things that she didn't want anyone to know about.

I was thankful for the times that I was left with Nana and other whānau. My little sister Katie and older brother Shaun weren't so lucky. They didn't get to stay at Nana's. They didn't get to know the whānau and Māori world like I did. To be Māori.

Nana was always happy to have me; however she wanted to see Katie and Shaun too. She'd complain about Mum never letting them stay.

Mum was protective of Katie and Shaun. 'I don't want them anywhere near those bloody marreys,' she'd say.

So my siblings missed out. Although under Mum's guidance they didn't see it that way.

It was strange arriving at Nana's house, knowing that Mum looked down on her and the whānau. It would take a while for Mum's voice in my head to go quiet before I could relax and enjoy my stay.

Mum's attitude towards Māori was a reflection of New Zealand white society at the time. Māori were seen as ignorant and backwards. While Mum may have married a brown boy, she didn't want to have anything to do with the Māori world.

An uncle told me that Mum was always uncomfortable around the whānau, always trying to take my dad—his cousin—away. He said that the day Mum came to meet the whānau at Aunty Nelly's house she wouldn't come inside, yet as a toddler I went straight in, got up on Uncle's lap at the dinner table and started eating the food from his plate. He said that at the time he and the other whānau at the table didn't know what to make of this little blond-haired, blue-eyed white boy. Apparently I blew them away.

¤ ¤ ¤

One of my aunties was called Aunty Joy. She was Poppa's sister. She stood over 6 foot and was known for knocking men out with a single punch. Aunty Joy Anderson was forever hugging and holding me. No one hurt children when Aunty Joy was around.

'There's my Timmy,' Aunty Joy would beam whenever she saw me, scooping me up in her strong arms.

Because of this, when anyone asked me as a toddler who I was I would say, 'My Timmy, me.'

At such a young age my answer made perfect sense to me. From then on I became known in the whānau as 'My Timmy me', and that is still the case today. In fact when I was re-connecting with whānau as a young man I went north to Rīpia Marae. Many of the older ones there were wondering who this Pākehā fella was. My Aunty Martha tried to explain to them how I fitted in, yet the old ones were still confused.

In the end Aunty said, 'It's Timmy me, My Timmy me.'

And that was it.

' Oh, of course,' the old ones sang. 'My Timmy me.'

'Where are your glasses, boy?'

'What happened to your blonde hair?'

They spoke to me as if I was still that little boy.

I looked at them. *I'm a man now*, I thought, standing tall.

'Timmy me,' they chuckled.

Embarrassed as I was, I am proud of the name My Timmy me. It has given me a sense of belonging and connection. It is my name within the whānau.

¤ ¤ ¤

Pākehā liked to point out to Dad that he wasn't my and Shaun's biological father—reminding him that we were white and he was brown. So one day Dad set out to brown us up. He lathered Shaun and me with coconut tanning oil and made us lie on towels out in the sun. Dad sat back on a beach chair next to us wearing only his underwear and shades.

Every now and then he told us to turn over so the sun could get our other side. We lay in the sun for ages, but we didn't brown. Dad got darker, but Shaun and I just burned bright red like a couple of crayfish. Then we blistered and peeled.

¤ ¤ ¤

On the other side of the family was Mum's mum, called Nanny by us kids. When I was young she lived in the Waitakere foothills. Nanny was a devout Christian attending church every Sunday. She would always be humming hymns.

When Shaun wasn't with Mum he was usually with Nanny. Apparently he was a favourite.

However sometimes the three of us—Shaun, Katie and I—would all stay at Nanny's place on weekends. The only sound at night in Nanny's house was the tick-tock of her grandfather clock. I loved going to sleep to the sound of that clock. In the morning I would wake up to Nanny humming in the kitchen. If us kids got out of bed early enough we would catch Nanny with her hair out. Her silver hair was so long it went past her bottom. She always kept it up in a bun, so it was a treat to see it out.

I got to enjoy the silence at Nanny's house. There was no television or radio at Nanny's — those were worldly, sinful things in the eyes of her church. Instead there were books, wooden blocks and Lego. None of us kids had ever seen Lego before Nanny showed us. One of Nanny's brothers had brought her a set back from Europe for her grandchildren to play with. If we behaved Nanny would bring the Lego box out from her bedroom and we would have a chance to play with it.

It wasn't easy to share since there weren't a lot of pieces to go around.

This made for a lot of arguments and fights. Whenever I was upset with Shaun or Katie, Nanny would make me stand in front of her.

'Look at my finger,' she'd say, holding it up in front of me.

I would look at her finger then up at her eyes. 'But...' I tried to argue.

'Look at my finger, Timothy,' Nanny continued, not giving me a chance to speak.

I didn't want to look at her finger. I just wanted her to hear my complaint about my brother and sister. However Nanny wouldn't let up. She kept telling me to look at her finger. It got to the point where I couldn't help but laugh at the absurdity of it.

'There, you see,' Nanny would say. 'It wasn't such a big deal after all, was it?'

I came to learn that this was how Mum's family dealt with problems. There was sexual and physical abuse going on within the family, yet no one wanted to know about it. They just wanted everything swept under the carpet and to pretend that life was great. If they didn't know the reality then it wasn't their problem—they weren't responsible and could plead ignorance. Whenever cracks started to appear, as they inevitably did, the family would dig in and stick to the rulebook—in other words stare at the finger.

Nanny was an amazing cook. Sponges were her specialty. She was also an avid reader. While we played games Nanny would sit in her chair consuming books. When it wasn't the *Bible* in her hands it was a *National Geographic* or a book on the natural world. Nanny also liked to read her brother Norman's poetry. Uncle Norman Frost wrote a lot, but never saw it as a profession. He was a Christian missionary based in India.

Nanny would sometimes share stories with us kids of Poppa and how he went AWOL from the army to be with her so many times that in the end the army kicked him out. Nanny would also tell of how she used to keep a bowl of pennies on the windowsill just to throw at Poppa whenever he turned up drunk, which apparently was quite often.

Nanny told me that I would be poorer than my siblings when I grew up.

'You'll be the poorest, Timmy,' she'd say. 'But you'll be the happiest.'

I didn't want to believe her. How can a poor person be happy? Yet as a young man I pursued community work and became a struggling author. I may be the poorest and I can say that I'm happy, but I don't know enough about my siblings' lives to know if I'm the happiest.

Mum had two sisters. I adored both of my aunties and their families. Mum's eldest sister lived in Hamilton, so we didn't get to see her much. The youngest sister lived on Swanson Road, directly across from Nana Tipene. It was strange staying on either side of Swanson Road and never crossing over to see the other family. They said it was because of the traffic and that they didn't want us kids going near the road, yet while both sides of the family were civil with one another, there was an invisible divide between the Pākehā and Māori parts of my family. A division I could never understand.

¤ ¤ ¤

I had problems with my eyes as a boy. Long-sighted, I was cross-eyed and had double vision. There were two lanes going down the North-Western Motorway at that time, but I was seeing four lanes and the same red car was in two of them.

As a result I had to have two eye operations. Both were traumatic. My eye trouble was one of the many reasons that I wasn't at school much. There were countless appointments at the eye clinic at Auckland Hospital, and periods of recovery required after each surgery.

My first stay in hospital was when I was five. I was terrified. I remember fighting a cold, uncaring nurse in the operating theatre. The stern old woman was trying to force a gas mask onto my face. I had both hands up pushing that mask back. However the nurse proved stronger than me, and I soon lost consciousness.

When I woke I couldn't open my eyes, yet I could tell that I was completely surrounded by family. I could feel them close to me and hear their voices. Their hands were on me. It wasn't Mum or Nanny or anyone else from my birth family. Nor was it Dad. None of them were there.

It was whānau. It was Nana, Aunty Nan Cleaver and my uncles. I tried to open my eyes to see them all, but couldn't. Panicking, I pulled at the bandages wrapped firmly around my head. Uncle Blake stopped me, and Nana and the others got me to calm down.

'You're okay, Timmy,' Nana said. 'Your eyes need to rest, boy. Just leave the bandage.'

I wanted so badly to see them all, but their voices and touching were the only reassurance I could get.

They had brought me chocolates, sweets and fruit, yet it was their love and connection that mattered most. I hadn't woken alone in the dark. My whānau had been there for me with their voices, their touch and their presence. I knew that I was alive because they affirmed my existence. They showed me that I mattered.

SINGLED OUT

For me, life with the whānau and life at home were two very different things. There is a saying in Māoridom that 'our children are our taonga'. With the whānau I felt loved and treasured. This was not the case with my immediate family. Behind closed doors there were unresolved demons.

A shadow hung over my childhood and teenage years. His name was Peter.

Peter was a convicted serial sex offender and paedophile who had spent a lot of time behind bars. His other charges included kidnapping, violent assault and threatening to kill, and he was my biological father. Mum had been married to Peter.

When my little sister, Katie, started school she got a hard time from the other children. Back then Whenuapai Primary School was predominantly full of white kids. As soon as they laid eyes on Katie with her brown skin they asked me, 'Why is your sister a different colour from you?'

I didn't know. I was eight and had forgotten about my life before the whānau. All I knew was that Katie was my sister. I didn't see colour.

That evening in my bedroom I asked Mum why Katie was brown and I was white. She explained to me that Dad wasn't my biological father, but that he was Katie's father.

I was shocked. 'Dad's my dad,' I said, scrunching beneath my covers.

'No, he's not,' Mum replied, standing at the edge of my bed with her arms crossed. 'He's your stepfather.'

'So where's my father?' I asked.

Mum told me that my father was Peter. 'He was a monster,' she said, and explained that Peter was in prison for hurting women and children. She said that he had hurt her.

I didn't know what to say.

Mum then said that I would grow up to be like Peter. She told me that I would be a monster and hurt women and children too.

I was horrified. 'No,' I exclaimed. 'I won't do that.'

'You won't be able to help it,' Mum stated, matter of fact. 'It's just who you are.'

'I won't do that, Mum!' I said, wanting her to know that I was good and worthy of her love.

But she just walked away.

Full of fear, I looked up at the ceiling. I didn't want to be a baddie, a monster, like those I watched on television shows. I wanted to be a goodie. I was eight years old and had just been told that my destiny was predetermined. That I was destined to hurt people. Wasn't there anything that could be done to change it? When people were sick they went to the doctor, when a car was broken it was fixed. Couldn't something be done to stop me from becoming a monster?

That incident wasn't the only time Mum laid out her prediction for me and my future. She made a point of reminding me of the monster I would become, while at the same time going into greater detail of what Peter had done to her. How he had knocked out some of her teeth. She also told me that my father had raped her and that it was from that rape that she had gotten pregnant with me. Mum held it over me as though I was the rape itself.

'You're gonna be a monster just like ya father!' she'd growl. 'You'll end up in prison, you'll see.'

Mum had been abused as a girl. Sexual abuse was rife in the family. A never-ending cycle that had come down the generations. When Mum met and married Peter she had only seen what she wanted to see. The romanticised imaginings of a young woman rather than the ugly reality.

Mum would later speak of walking in on Peter with the little girl from next door on their bed. The girl was dressed up in Mum's clothes. Choosing not see it, Mum turned around and exited the room, closing the door behind her and leaving the child to her fate.

However, as much as Mum had tried to keep the past behind a closed door it had a way of seeping out. She had been traumatised. As well as hurt, she had anger and resentment, and this she projected onto others. Mum couldn't be close to me without feeling uncomfortable.

One morning I heard crying. I walked into the lounge to find Mum huddled up on the couch with Shaun and Katie. The three of them were in tears. I was around five or six years old. Alarmed, I approached them.

'Don't you dare!' Mum yelled. 'Don't you come near us. It's all your fault.'

The three of them looked at me as though I had done the worst thing imaginable.

'Dad's leaving and it's all your fault!' Mum spat. 'Go away!'

Alone and rejected, I returned to my room. I had no idea what I had done. All I knew was that I was to blame for Mum's pain. I found out when I was older that Dad had told Mum that he was leaving her and going to live in Australia. Dad had only said it to get a reaction.

Mum's life was as dramatic as the daytime soaps she clung to, such as *Days of our Lives* and *The Young and the Restless*. Mum couldn't handle a settled life. Whenever it was too quiet she would find a way to rev it up. Anything to avoid the lingering effects of her past. Dad was no different.

One afternoon Dad was sitting on the floor in the hallway. He was on the phone arguing with Mum, who was at work. When he hung the phone up the house was quiet.

'Shaun?' Dad called.

My older brother was quick to respond. 'Yes, Dad,' he said.

'Get the large knife out of the kitchen drawer and put it on the table,' Dad instructed.

Suddenly the house felt eerie.

I got off my bed and looked out from my room. I knew something was wrong. Little Katie felt it too. She stood up from playing on the lounge floor.

Shaun dutifully placed the knife on the dining table. Dad sighed as he stood up. He crossed the lounge.

As Dad reached to pick up the knife Katie started to cry.

'We love you, Daddy,' Katie and Shaun both said.

Dad dropped to his knees and Katie and Shaun rushed to hug him. I watched from my bedroom as the three of them held each other, crying. I knew it wasn't safe for me to go out there. Especially when there was a knife around.

I was an outsider in my family. I even looked different being the only one with blonde hair and blue eyes. My parents and siblings all had dark hair and brown eyes.

Shaun was Mum's first born. Mum had him with Peter in the beginning of their relationship, the honeymoon period. When they split up Mum and Peter fought over custody of Shaun. Katie was the only girl and Dad's only child, and again she came during a romantic time. I came at a darker point in Mum's life and not in a good way. There was no custody battle over me. To Mum I even look like Peter.

That's not to say that Shaun and Katie weren't hurt. In my family everyone got hurt, just some less than others. I was seen as the black sheep and singled out. Not because I did anything wrong. Just because I was there.

When Mum, Shaun and Katie were on Grafton Bridge in Auckland City late at night, all trying to talk Dad down from jumping, I was made to stay in the car because my words had no sway. It was the same when Dad, Shaun and Katie were trying to stop Mum from jumping out of the moving car on the motorway.

One night when I was small I'd had enough. I said to Mum that I wanted to run away. Mum got me dressed, put me outside in the dark and shut the door. As I banged and cried on the door, begging for Mum to let me back in, she and Shaun were laughing at me from inside.

Sometimes Mum liked to get the family to give me the silent treatment. No one would talk to me—not Mum, Dad, Shaun or Katie. They would completely ignore me. If I tried to talk to them they would walk away. It wasn't for an hour, or for an afternoon, or even a day. It lasted for days. There were times where I wondered if I even existed.

Mum had strict rules for Dad. He wasn't to hit Katie or Shaun, but he could do what he liked to me. I was the devil's spawn as far as Mum was concerned.

Dad's experience with the whanau was different to mine. He spoke a lot about the violence and abuse he'd endured as a kid. No matter how hard he dished it out to me he would always say that he'd had it worse. Whenever the whānau was nice to me Dad became more hostile. It was as though he resented their love for me. And so I became the target of Dad's projections as well.

I adored Mum and Dad. They may have been hurting me, but I wanted their love and acceptance so much that I was willing to overlook any abuse. Everyone wants to believe they are a part of a loving and caring family, just like the ones on television. It is touted as the normal. If you are not part of the pack you don't survive. Yet Mum and Dad were damaged people, and the more I chased them the more they pushed me away.

When I was in my early twenties Dad confronted me in the kitchen with a knife. 'If I ever see you again I'll fuckin kill you!' he spat.

Katie stood beside me, crying. 'Why are you doing this to Timmy?' she yelled. 'Why have you always done this to my brother?'

Dad ignored her.

I hadn't done anything wrong. Dad and Mum had left home and gone their separate ways. They had wanted me home at this stage to keep an eye on the house and on Katie and her baby. Now, though, they were making changes and wanted me out, and not just of the house.

Dad glared at me. 'You have never been a part of this family,' he said through gritted teeth. 'And you never will be. You're no son of mine!'

'Stop it, Dad!' Katie cried. 'Don't do this!'

Dad pointed at me with the blade. 'You get the fuck out of this house, and don't you ever come back here again,' he said. 'If I see you walking on the road I'll fuckin run you over. I'm telling ya, boy, if I see you again, I'll kill you.'

To be singled out and mistreated hurt, and I carried the projections that my parents put on me for the greater part of my life, and they affected and influenced every aspect of my life. However, it is said that to understand ourselves we must understand our parents. While it had felt personal the guilt, shame and self loathing was never mine to own. My family has been plagued with never ending cycles of generational abuse. The individuals and relationships are complex. Everyone has their own story, hurt and shame, and I'm not the only one to be treated as different and singled out.

To this day I love my parents and only want the best for them. In acknowledging the abuse I endured I shine a light on their suffering and the suffering of all my family. No one is born a monster. Monsters are man-made. It would take me some time to learn this, that everyone who hurt me had been hurt themselves.

HOME WAS A SCARY PLACE

Darkness was all I could see as I looked out from the door of the lit bathroom. I looked back at the toilet. I could try and go again. Anything would be better than having to walk through the dark to my bedroom. But too much going back and forth would only attract his attention.

My fingers rested on the light switch. I knew that as soon as I turned it off I was committed to going to bed.

Perhaps tonight will be different, I thought. *Perhaps he's already in bed.*

I turned off the light and moved swiftly through the blackened kitchen, but when I reached the lounge I felt him coming at me. Dad picked me up and threw me across the lounge. I crashed into an armchair, tipping it over. I knew that would make him angrier.

'I'm sorry, Dad,' I said, as he gripped me again.

This time I landed against the wall.

Dad came at me, thumping and punching. I could feel his disgust and rage, see it etched across his shadowed face. He grabbed me and the abuse continued. These moments were often soaked in the smell of alcohol, but not always. I was a little kid and I was powerless. This was my life. I knew no different.

Mum was at work. She worked at a burger bar in Henderson in the evenings. Mum liked parties so some nights she wouldn't come home until well into the morning. She would sometimes find me curled up sleeping on the bathroom floor next to the toilet. I hadn't had the nerve to walk through the dark on those nights. Mum would send me to bed.

One afternoon I approached Mum in the kitchen.

'Mum,' I said. 'Mrs Battersby wants me to show you the lump under my arm.'

Hearing my year seven teacher's name, Mum knew this was something she couldn't dismiss.

I pulled up my shirt and showed her the lump in the pit of my arm.

Mum frowned. 'Where did you get that?' she asked.

'Dad did it,' I said.

'Rubbish!' Mum grumbled. 'Your father didn't do that to you.'

'Yes, he did,' I argued, deciding to put it all on the line.

Mrs Battersby had seen the lump under my arm and couldn't believe that a mother would allow her child to be treated in such a way. She had encouraged me to go home and to show Mum. Mrs Battersby was certain that Mum would do the right thing.

With my caring teacher on my side I felt empowered and brave. 'Dad beats me up every night when you're at work,' I said.

'You're telling Mrs Battersby lies!' Mum growled.

'Ask Shaun,' I argued.

'Shaun!' Mum called him out of his bedroom.

I looked at my older brother as he appeared. Was he going to leave me in the lurch or was he going to have my back? For as long as I could remember Shaun had lived in his room, behind his closed door. He hardly ever came out, shutting himself away from all the drama and the violence. Shaun was Mum's special boy. The abuse and violence was never aimed at him. But he knew what was going on. He would hear my cries, hear me being thrown against the wall, hear Dad's rage, and sometimes Shaun was right there, helplessly watching it play out in front of him.

'Your brother's gone and opened his big mouth to Mrs Battersby at school,' Mum said. She pointed at the lump and bruising under my arm. 'Did Dad do that to Timmy?' she asked.

I knew Shaun had had a good experience with Mrs Battersby when she'd been his teacher. I hoped that since she was involved he would now have the strength to speak up too.

'Yes,' Shaun said. 'Dad did that to Tim.'

'Did you see him do it?' Mum queried further.

'Yes,' Shaun replied.

'I don't believe it,' Mum muttered. 'I'll ask your father about it when he comes home.'

The next night Dad called me into the lounge. His first hit sent me across the room.

'It wasn't just me!' I cried. 'Shaun told Mum too!'

I pointed at Shaun's room where he was hiding behind his closed door.

But this wasn't about Shaun. Nor was it about me telling Mum. This was about me telling Mrs Battersby.

'You shut your fuckin mouth, boy!' Dad yelled.

He then showed me that I was his ragdoll and that he could do whatever he wanted to me.

'You talk too much,' Mum said to me the next day. 'You need to learn to keep your mouth shut.'

From then on Mum adopted the phrase, 'Timmy's got a big mouth.'

I didn't want to see things as they really were. I didn't want to see how alone I was. I wanted to believe that Mum wasn't part of the abuse. I was desperate to have something good in my life. Perhaps not wanting to see my life for what it was could have been why I had so much trouble with my eyes.

I wore glasses for much of my childhood and, much to the annoyance and anger of my parents, I went through a number of pairs.

One time I was out on my Uncle Todd's boat fishing up at Leigh. Uncle Todd was Mum's wealthy white brother-in-law. His kids—my cousins—were much older than me and they were forever getting me to do the wrong thing because it brought them great amusement.

One cousin, Daniel, kept getting me to look over the side of his Dad's boat. I didn't know why, but then my glasses fell off my face. Daniel and I could only watch as the glasses slowly sank out of sight into the depths of the ocean. We looked at one another.

Uncle Todd noticed. 'What?' he queried.

'Timmy's glasses fell into the water,' Daniel said.

Everyone looked at my face. The only sound was the water slapping against the side of the boat.

'A fish will be wearing your glasses now, Timmy,' Daniel joked, trying to make light of the situation. The people on board the boat laughed, but Dad wasn't laughing.

He shook his head and looked away. He would deal with me later when no one was around.

One day at school some boys ran off with my glasses. I chased them all over the field. For the boys it was a game of piggy in the middle. They tossed my glasses back and forth to one another while I frantically ran around in a mad panic trying to get them.

The game ended when my glasses collided with a steel bar on the playground. The boys ran off laughing as I picked my glasses up. My heart sank as I discovered that the top of the glasses frame had snapped on one side and a lens had fallen out.

I ran to my classroom and found my teacher. I told her what had happened and showed her my glasses. The look of horror on her face reflected how I was feeling inside.

'Oh no, Timothy,' she said.

She hugged me.

My teacher sat down at a desk. She spread glue on the edges of the broken frame, put the lens back in and re-joined my glasses. After wiping away any evidence of the glue my teacher then added a little sellotape for extra support. When she had finished it was hard to tell the glasses were broken at all. The teacher was obviously counting on the fact that my parents didn't pay close attention to me, so they wouldn't notice finer details.

'I don't know how long it's going to last, Timothy,' she said, returning the glasses to my face. She said that it would buy me some time though. She told me to look for an opportunity to get rid of the glasses without it being my fault, so I wouldn't get into trouble.

Unfortunately, the opportunity didn't come.

A few days later it was Katie's birthday. Mum, Dad and Shaun were sitting on the floor in the lounge watching Katie open her presents. I was standing beside Dad, looking down, when the lens dropped from my glasses and landed on the floor right beside his hand. My heart dropped as he and Mum both looked at the lens. When Dad's eyes lifted to meet mine his face was already full of rage.

'You fuckin little bastard,' Mum snarled.

There was no chance to explain. Mum and Dad were quick to get up from the floor and I got a hiding.

The beatings always hurt. When Dad hit it was a thump or a punch. Mum preferred to thump or to use whatever was close by, like the broom or the vacuum cleaner pipe. She once drew blood on Shaun's leg with her high-heel shoe. Neither of them used an open hand.

Yet this time, although the hits hurt they couldn't take away the feeling I had inside. The feeling that I wasn't alone. My teacher had tried to patch up my glasses in order to buy me some time and protect me from my parents' anger.

To witness my teacher's first reaction at the sight of my broken glasses, and then the way she had tried to mend them, demonstrated to me her concern, her understanding. Teachers knew what was happening in my home. Sadly, I was too young to remember this teacher's name but while her attempts to save me from a beating hadn't worked out, I have always remembered that she tried, and that she was willing to be with me in that secret shadow world where abuse dwells. That teacher lit up the darkness just a little – enough that I can still see it brightly. I knew that I wasn't alone. One person, one act can make a difference.

A HUNK OF WOOD

'Timmy!' Mum yelled.

I came out of my bedroom and into the lounge.

Mum was sitting with Katie on the couch. Katie was wiping her eyes.

'What's going on at school?' Mum asked.

I looked at Katie and shrugged. 'I don't know.'

'Kids are teasing your sister!' Dad growled.

I couldn't understand why they were so upset with me. I hadn't teased her. I had been trying hard to keep my head down and stay out of trouble—I'd already been dealt with for fighting at school.

It turned out that kids had been telling Katie she'd been rolling in the mud and that's why she was brown.

'Why aren't you looking after your sister?' Mum snapped.

I looked at Shaun's room. I had figured it was his job to look after Katie since he was the eldest and most responsible. He was already carrying Katie's bag home from the bus stop each day.

'If anyone is mean to your sister you beat them up, you hear?' Mum said. 'If you don't you'll get it from us when you get home.'

I was confused. Mum had told me not to fight after the school complained about me, and now she was telling me to fight.

'If you don't do it, boy, we'll hear about it,' Dad said.

Mum and Dad were limited in their ability to address problems. They weren't willing to front up to the school and speak to them about Katie being picked on—they wouldn't have known how to or had the emotional competency to do so. There was also a perception within the family that we were seen as different and looked down on. Katie wasn't the only one of us to be treated as an outsider by the community.

So the only response Mum or Dad had was to lash out.

From that point on Katie knew she had muscle at school. Whenever she had trouble with kids she would come running to me. I was more afraid of my parents than I was of the school, so I would rush in with both fists swinging. The power went to Katie's head and she started to tease and provoke kids, sometimes the biggest kids in the school. She would make them chase after her and then lead them right to me.

'Timmy, remember what Mum and Dad said,' she'd say as some big kid was bearing down on me.

¤ ¤ ¤

I was a scrapper at school until I met Miss Foote. I loved and adored my year 6 teacher so much I was set on marrying her. In Miss Foote's class I excelled and my behaviour improved.

One day when Miss Foote was sitting beside me she looked at me and simply said, 'I don't like fighting, Timothy.'

Instantly there was a click in my brain. *I will never fight again*, I thought to myself.

Of course choosing not to fight was going directly against Mum and Dad. I would get a hiding if I didn't beat up any kid who messed with Katie. But I didn't care anymore. It didn't matter what I did — good choices, bad choices or simply nothing at all — I still got hidings, and I would happily take the hidings at home for Miss Foote.

This was put to the test one lunchtime when a senior boy climbed up a tree just outside our classroom and pushed out a bird's nest, killing the chicks. As a class we had been studying the baby birds' progress. Miss Foote really cared about animals; she cared about everything.

Girls from my class came and found me. Me and my mates were misfits at school. We stuck together, and anyone who picked on us got beaten up. My best friend was Vincent. He was Tongan and, like my sister, was one of only a few brown kids at our school.

Our reputation as enforcers was well known, and kids who felt bullied would turn to us for help and protection. We were only too happy to help because it not only kept bullies away from us—we also got to play the heroes.

The girls from my class told me what the boy had done to the nest of birds. We all knew Miss Foote would be upset about it. *We* were upset. As I approached the boy I suddenly thought, *What am I going to do? I'm not fighting anymore. I can't let Miss Foote down.*

The boy and his mates were sitting on a seat outside their classroom and looking all smug while arguing with other girls from my class.

'They killed the birds, Tim,' one of the girls said as I walked up.

'Why did you do that?' I asked.

Normally I wouldn't have said anything. I would have just jumped in with fists flying.

'What are you going to do about it?' the boy taunted.

I wasn't sure what to do. This was new. What does one do in these situations if you're not going to throw a fist?

'You should have left the birds alone,' I said, putting my hand on the boy's shoulder.

It was the move the senior boy had been waiting for. Perhaps he knew of me and my reputation, because his fist led the way as he jumped up.

Wham! He punched me straight in the eye.

I fell back.

The boy stood with his fists at the ready, waiting for my reply.

But as much as I wanted to hit him, I couldn't stop thinking about Miss Foote.

Seeing that I wasn't going to come back at him, the boy and his friends laughed and walked away. The girls were looking confused, wondering where the old Tim had gone.

When Miss Foote found out she was furious. She took me by the hand, marched me into the older boy's classroom and showed the teacher, Mr Wallace, my blackening eye. 'Look what your student did to Timothy,' Miss Foote said.

'It's about time someone gave Timothy a taste of his own medicine,' Mr Wallace smiled.

His class laughed.

Miss Foote's face burnt red. 'Timothy is making changes,' she argued. 'He tried to do the right thing. Your student pushed a bird's nest out of a tree, killing the chicks.'

Mr Wallace couldn't care less. He was condescending towards the much younger Miss Foote. He continued to mock her, making his class laugh even more.

How dare you treat Miss Foote like this? I thought, eyeballing him.

'Come on, Timothy,' Miss Foote said, 'we're not getting anywhere here.'

I could have told her that before we even set foot in that classroom. Miss Foote was a sincere, genuine and caring person, but there were few teachers like her. The majority of teachers I knew couldn't care less about a kid like me.

While I had lost the fight it turned out that I was a winner.

For the remainder of the afternoon Miss Foote had me lie down on the pillows in the reading corner, where she sat beside me, held me in her arms and gently rubbed my head. I was in heaven.

'How are you feeling now, Timothy?' Miss Foote would ask.

'Ooooh,' I'd say, clutching my eye and never wanting the moment to end.

¤ ¤ ¤

One morning Dad noticed that I was reluctant to go to school.

'What's your problem?' he gruffly asked.

'I don't want to go to school today,' I said.

His frown deepened. 'Why not?'

I tried to explain to Dad that I had had an argument with my best friend Vincent.

'We're going to fight,' I said. I don't want to fight him.'

Dad glared at me. 'You go to school!' He pointed at the door. 'You pick up a hunk of wood, and you whack that boy across the head with it!'

I was quiet.

Vincent and his family had been good to me and my family. They had invited us to their family events. Vincent and his brother, Alex, respected Dad. Alex had even come around one afternoon and washed Dad's motorbike. Yet Dad didn't like Vincent or his family, and he didn't like me hanging out with them. Being Māori, Dad had experienced racism, and in turn had become anti towards other ethnic groups. In many ways he was even anti Māori. The world had told Dad that anything not white was bad and Dad had bought into it. I believe at times he hated himself most of all.

'And if you don't whack that boy across the head,' Dad growled, 'I'm going to give you a hiding when you get home!'

I looked at Dad and thought, *There's something wrong with you. There's something not right in your head.*

I knew what it felt like to be hurt. There was no way that I was going to go to school, pick up a hunk of wood and whack a person across the head with it. I knew nothing good would come from doing something like that. Vincent would be hurt, I would be in trouble and the school would be phoning home.

At the time Dad was doing shift work, often working through the night. When he was home he was usually asleep so I managed to avoid him for the next few days. In the end I didn't have to tell him that I hadn't whacked Vincent with a hunk of wood and he never asked about it.

Like any friendship, Vincent and I had our ups and downs—especially when I broke his toy Robot and was an egg about it—but we never came to blows and I was pleased with my decision to never let Miss Foote down.

GOODBYE TO THE WHĀNAU

My life was full of whānau and hui when I was small. Someone always seemed to be getting married or having a birthday. There was always an occasion to celebrate with lots of food, music and dance, and lots of drinking and smoking. At parties, when I wasn't dancing or mucking around with my cousins outside in the dark I would get under the table where my aunties were playing cards. I felt safe under there away from my parents. At other times there were gatherings around a fire with guitars and singing. As well as joy and laughter there were tears and sadness too. It seemed like every second day I was with whānau. They were even picking me up from school.

But over time that started to change.

Dad and Mum liked to complain about the whānau, said they were all, 'bloody horis'. Mum couldn't stand the snoring at the marae and didn't like the Māori way of living—she craved a more refined way of life.

She was set on *improving* our lives. At first it was small things, like the clothes Dad wore and the food we ate. Then there was no more going to the races or the TAB. With each small change came another.

I badly wanted to play rugby. I saw it as a way to connect with Dad — I believed that if I excelled at rugby that I could win him over.

However Mum put a stop to rugby. Apparently Dad was even up for All Black selection, but Mum wasn't having it. There were no more rugby games and no more clubrooms. While I was chasing the love and approval of my parents, Dad was chasing Mum's. He was like a little boy around her. He couldn't settle unless she was home.

After being abused in her childhood and first marriage, Mum was now choosing to be with a man she could control and manipulate — and she played Dad like a puppet.

During these changes Dad found out that he was whangai (adopted by a relative), and he was the last to know. His favourite aunty, who had passed away, turned out to be his biological mother. Dad felt betrayed and wronged by Nana, Poppa and the whānau. He resented them, and still carries that resentment to this day.

Of course there was more to the story, but Dad didn't want to hear it. From that point on we weren't to have anything to do with Nana Tipene. We were becoming isolated and disconnected from the whānau.

¤ ¤ ¤

When I was eight Mum had her first encounter with cervical cancer. Her friend was diagnosed around the same time as her, and her friend didn't make it. Mum got scared, realising there was a possibility that she might not survive. But she wasn't only scared about dying—she'd been brought up through her mother's church, and she was now thinking she was on a one-way ticket straight to hell. It was time for more changes.

So it was goodbye to worldly influences like the television and radio, goodbye to the last of the whānau and old friends, and off to church we went. We were now born-again Christians, and life became surreal as Mum and Dad tried to alter everything about them.

One Sunday morning I got up early to use the toilet. As I walked through the kitchen I could smell Mum's baking from the night before. Mum was a good cook when she wanted to be, and right now I was smelling ginger crunch.

On the way back from the bathroom I decided to take a peek. I lifted up the tea towel and eyed the ginger crunch in the baking dish. It had been covered and left out for the icing to set. The ginger icing looked so good. Surely if I ran my finger through it no one would know it was me? I knew I would get a hiding if I got caught, but even though I was afraid of hidings I was very much used to them.

I looked around. No one else was up yet. I ran a finger through the icing and put it into my mouth. It was sweet and yum. I looked at the ginger crunch with a finger groove running through it. If my plan worked what difference would another finger groove make? They still wouldn't know that it was me.

I ran my finger through it again, and again, and again. I gave up using one finger and instead ran all four fingers across the top of the ginger crunch, scooping up the icing and putting it into my mouth. When I had finished the crunch was covered in groove marks. It didn't look good. I knew I'd gone too far, but it was too late now. I covered the pan with the tea towel and went back to my room. I sat on my bed and sucked the remainder of the ginger icing from my fingers. There was nothing else to do but to wait, anxiously.

Later that morning it happened.

'Who's been into the ginger crunch?' Mum growled from the kitchen. 'Look what they've done,' she said, obviously showing Dad.

I couldn't see. I was hiding in my bedroom.

Each of us kids were asked if we had done it.

'No, I didn't,' I called out, echoing the words of my brother and sister.

'Right,' Mum said. 'Well, there's an easy way to find out. Let's see whose fingers fit into the grooves.'

Oops, I hadn't thought of that.

Katie was called up first.

'Put your fingers in the pan, Katie, and we'll see if they're the same size as the grooves,' Mum explained. 'No, your fingers are too small.'

It was then Shaun's turn.

I was being left till last.

'Put your fingers into the grooves, Shaun, and let's see if it was you,' Mum said. 'No, your fingers are too big.'

In my mind I was pleading for the phone to ring or for there to be a knock at the door. Anything to take Mum's attention away from the ginger crunch.

'Timothy, come here,' Mum called. 'It's your turn.'

Mum, Dad, Shaun and Katie all watched me as I came out of my room and into the kitchen.

'Let's see if your fingers fit,' Mum said.

They knew that it was me who'd defaced the ginger crunch and eaten the icing. But Mum wanted to play it out like a scene from *Goldilocks and the Three Bears*.

I put my fingers into the icing, hoping for a miracle that they wouldn't fit the grooves.

'A perfect fit,' Mum said. 'Go to your room. Your father will be in to see you.'

I sat on my bed and waited for my punishment. I knew it was going to hurt; it always did. There was no telling what he would do or what he would use, because there were a variety of ways that he used to beat me. When he entered the room I jumped to my feet and braced for the impact.

Dad closed the door behind him and sat on my bed.

I figured he was messing with me, setting me up.

But this time Dad didn't lash out. Instead he talked to me. He never raised his voice, he didn't yell or roar. He didn't threaten me or put me down. His face wasn't all screwed up. Instead Dad was calm and he spoke to me softly.

He told me that what I'd done wasn't right, and that I shouldn't do it again. After he'd spoken he opened his arms and told me to come to him.

Here we go, I thought, shutting my eyes tight and bracing for impact.

Yet Dad surprised me further by hugging me.

It was an awkward hug, forced and weird. It wasn't loving or sincere.

He asked if I was all right.

'Yes.' I nodded.

Then Dad got up and walked out, closing the door behind him.

I was left standing in the middle of my room, confused. I had no idea what was going on.

Was it over? Was he going to come back because he'd forgotten what he'd come into my room for? Was Mum coming in? Was she going to be the one to dish out the hits this time? Were they just messing with my head as they often did?

I stayed standing just in case. However nothing happened. I was left in my room.

It was a one-off. Dad and Mum had never addressed my behaviour like this before, and they never did it again.

I missed the whānau—my grandmother, aunties, uncles and cousins.

At least we still got to see Uncle Blake because he was also pulling away from the whānau.

I liked staying with Uncle Blake. I worshiped him. Whenever I had the chance I would hang out with him. There were times it was just the two of us, and I would sit in his car and wait while he was in the TAB.

Uncle Blake liked to have us kids on. He would get us to wash his car and promised to pay us. So off we would go outside with buckets, brushes, rags and the hose. When we had finished we would race inside and tell him. Uncle Blake would take us back outside so he could inspect our work. He would then go around the car, pointing out any dirty spots that we had missed, and deduct money from us for each spot he found.

'Oh,' he'd say, 'look, there's another spot that you missed. That's 20 cents off.'

In the end we owed him money.

It was never left there though. Uncle Blake would take us kids down the road and buy us a big feed of fish 'n' chips, or lollies, crisps and fizzy drink.

When my rugby ball got stolen from the lawn of Uncle Blake's house in Ranui he let me stay up late and choose a drink from the top shelf in his drink cabinet. I wasn't keen on the taste of alcohol so I just went with a fizzy drink.

I got to go to Uncle's rugby games on Saturdays, and then to the clubrooms after. When he played rugby at the Waitematā Club my aunty and I would be in the stand with their sons. It was hard to look over at Nana's house and know she was so close.

Aunty must have noticed one day because she said, 'Now, boy, your grandmother's house is just over there. I know your mum and dad don't want you kids to see her but it's up to you. You can go see her if you want. I'm not saying you should, and I'm not saying you shouldn't. But if you choose to go I won't tell your parents.'

That was all that I needed to hear. I ran to Nana's house and got to see her and my uncles.

¤ ¤ ¤

Being home alone was normal for us kids. Mum and Dad were hardly ever there.

One afternoon Katie and I were mucking about in the house waiting for the rest of our family to turn up. I was eight and Katie was five. Shaun wasn't home—he often stayed over with Nanny, Mum's mum.

As night crept in Katie and I started to wonder if anyone was coming home. It was late when the phone rang. I answered it.

A woman asked to speak to Mum.

'She's not home,' I said.

'Is there another adult there that I could talk to?' the woman inquired.

'No.'

'So who is home with you?' the woman queried further.

'Just me and my little sister,' I said.

The woman asked some more questions then said goodbye. Katie and I went back to mucking around. A short time later the phone rang again. It was the same woman.

She said she was a nurse phoning from the hospital. Dad had been in a motorbike accident and the woman needed to know where Mum was.

'I don't know where she is,' I replied.

The lady asked if I knew the name of our neighbours.

My mind suddenly went blank. 'Mr Grassick,' I said, trying to remember.

The woman got me to repeat the name. She then said goodbye and hung up. When I got off the phone I realised I had given the nurse the wrong name. Mrs Tantell was our neighbour, not Mr Grassick. Old Mr Grassick ran the Herald Island store with his wife and son, Eddie. Mr Grassick lived some distance up Ferry Parade. I had gotten the names mixed up.

A short time later there was a knock at the door. I opened it and found Mr Grassick standing on the porch with a blanket under his arm. He came into the house. As it was late Mr Grassick put my sister and me to bed and then set up a bed for himself on the couch.

Mum woke me in the morning. She was furious. Furious that I had answered the phone and spoken to the nurse from the hospital, and furious that I had given the nurse Mr Grassick's name. Being the local store owner, Mr Grassick knew everyone's business.

'Now everybody's going to know,' Mum growled at me. 'Next time keep your bloody mouth shut! And why didn't you get you and your sister some dinner?'

Questions had obviously been asked about my and Katie's welfare.

'I didn't know what to cook,' I said, still hungry from the night before.

It turned out that the hospital kept trying to find Mum, but couldn't. My uncle, Mum's brother inlaw, eventually tracked her down. He found her at a house in bed with another man. Mum was embarrassed.

Dad was pretty messed up after the accident but it wasn't anything too serious. He'd been having some drinks after work and decided he'd try and pull some stunts on his motorbike. He ended up crashing.

¤ ¤ ¤

One day I was made to stay home from school. I was nine. A bag was packed for me and I was told to get into the car. It was just me and Dad. We drove from Herald Island to Auckland City. During the trip Dad never said a word to me, which wasn't unusual. The only time Dad ever spoke to me was when he was having a go.

I had an inkling of where we were going, but I was hoping I was wrong. It turned out I wasn't. We came to the grey, gloomy building I had come to know well: Auckland Hospital.

Dad parked in the Auckland Domain and we walked around to the entrance, got in the lift and went up some floors. Remembering my first eye operation when I was five, I was petrified. Since then I had come back to the hospital regularly for eye exams, but I'd never brought a packed bag. I was desperately hoping the bag meant I was going to be staying at somebody's place, like my wonderful Aunty Joy who lived in Otara. But I hadn't seen Aunty Joy in ages.

I followed Dad out of the lift and up to reception, where Dad spoke a little to a nurse behind the counter. The nurse led us through an adult ward and into a room in the children's ward. There was no one in it. I was shown to a bed in the corner. A sense of dread came over me.

'You're staying here,' Dad said.

He went to walk away, but I grabbed onto him and cried. I didn't want to stay there—I wanted to go home.

Dad smiled at the nurse as he pushed me back. 'You'll be right,' he said. 'We'll be in to see you.'

And with that he was gone.

I sat on the bed. I found my pencils and scrapbook in my bag so I took it out to draw in.

I was expecting a lonely night, but that didn't happen. A group of young nurses took an interest in me and spent much of their shift coming and going, making sure I was all right. They carried me around on their backs, drew pictures in my scrapbook and played with me. I forgot about my fear and felt a lot better. Those nurses were angels.

The next day I began to explore the hospital, going up and down the lifts, talking to nurses and adult patients, all the while avoiding the stern matron.

I knew all about matrons from my first operation. Back then I'd been placed in a similar ward to the one I was in this time, though that one had been full of children. When I was given my evening meal it had come with its own individual salt and pepper shakers. I was amazed. I was five years old and no one had trusted me with salt and pepper shakers before. I suddenly felt a sense of independence and freedom. I proceeded to put salt and pepper on my meal, and since I was allowed do this, I did it again and again.

The matron burst through the door, growling at me, and marched up the room past all the other children, whose eyes were wide with fear.

She snatched up the tray with my meal on it. 'If you're going to play with your food,' the matron snapped, 'then you don't get to eat it!'

The matron then marched off out of the room. I'd had every intention of eating my dinner. I was hungry. From then on I knew to stay away from the matrons.

When I returned from my exploration of Auckland Hospital I found I was no longer the only one in the children's ward. A Māori boy had moved in, taking the bed opposite me, against the window. We were around the same age and hit it off straight away. It was now the two of us exploring the hospital.

On the fifth of November us two boys sat on the bed by the window and watched the fireworks in the night sky over Auckland City. We had a good view from our floor, high in the hospital. I had been in hospital for a couple of days now. As I looked out the window I thought about my family out there enjoying their fireworks. My roommate had had visitors. His mum, dad and family had come to see him a lot, bringing him sweets and things which he shared with me. I hadn't had any visitors.

I was guessing that none of the whānau knew I was in hospital again.

¤ ¤ ¤

The morning of my operation came. The matron was on hand to ensure I got my injection in the backside.

'Right,' she said, getting me back under the covers. 'Now you are to stay in bed. No more running around the hospital. This injection will put you to sleep. If you run around it won't work and you'll have to have the gas.'

I cringed, remembering fighting the nurse with the gas mask before my first operation. I didn't want to experience that again.

The matron raised a finger. 'Stay in bed,' she commanded. She then left the ward.

I looked over at my roommate who was sitting on the edge of his bed, swinging his legs.

'Let's go,' he said.

He didn't have to tell me twice. The last thing I wanted to do was stay in bed, dreading the encroaching operation. I was frightened enough as it was. We sneaked out of the ward and off through the hospital.

We played in the lifts, sending items up and down and visiting every floor. We got lost in different rooms and corridors, and then found our way back to familiar places. We gave each other rides in a wheelchair. We visited adult patients and got fruit and sweets. We sat on the bed of one old Māori man and he played us songs on his guitar, played cards with us and told jokes to make us laugh.

Later in the day I was caught.

'There you are!' the matron growled. 'We've been looking all over for you!'

I was given a stern telling off as I was led back to my bed.

'You've ruined the anaesthetic,' the Matron grumbled. 'You obviously ran it off. You'll have to have the gas now.'

I eyed the door, wondering how I was going to get away this time. But there was no avoiding the operation. I was wheeled on the bed down corridors and into a lift, then wheeled through another corridor before entering a room with large lights and people in surgical gowns.

I didn't want to be in this room. This was the place where I had fought the nurse years before.

'Right, I need you to breathe nice and deep for me,' a nurse said from behind her surgical mask as she held me firmly with one hand.

I looked for her other hand, but couldn't see it. I couldn't see the gas mask either. Before I knew what was happening she had whisked it out from behind her and pushed it onto my face. My hands went straight up, my fingers clawing at the sides of the mask as I fought to get it off. But once again the nurse proved stronger than I was.

When I woke in hospital I was alone. There was no whānau surrounding me as there had been after my first operation.

I felt groggy. Only one eye was covered this time so I could look around. I couldn't see my roommate, and guessed he was either off exploring or having his own operation. It was a quiet day for me, lying in bed. I wasn't allowed to look at books or draw since that might strain the one eye that wasn't covered.

Fortunately my roommate turned up later and sat chatting with me.

¤ ¤ ¤

On the day I was to be discharged I was woken by a commotion early in the morning. My roommate was being wheeled out on his bed. I knew what that meant—it was time for his operation.

When I woke again later that morning he was being wheeled back in. His head was now half-covered in a bandage like mine. He was unconscious. I watched him for a while, wondering when he was going to wake up. I felt for him. He had been so full of life the day before, laughing and playing around. Now he was so quiet. I must have been the same for him.

When Mum came to pick me up my roommate was awake but drowsy, and he was surrounded by family. Mum was in a rush so I didn't get to say goodbye to him. He had been a good friend. I'm glad we had been there for one another.

Mum took me to her younger sister's place on Swanson Road, across the road from Nana Tipene. I was told to stay there and not to cross the road to see Nana. I stayed with my aunty and uncle for some time to recover from the operation. They were nice to me.

There was no going to school. I was under strict instructions from the doctors—no books, no television, no drawing. Nothing that would strain my uncovered eye.

Those were long days. I would look over the road at Nana's house and wonder if she knew I was so close. I missed the whānau.

THE PERCEPTIONS OF OTHERS

I felt sorry for our neighbours on Herald Island. They copped a lot from Mum and Dad. I recall one afternoon where Mum was encouraging my older cousins to bombard the neighbour's roof with watermelon skins while Uncle Todd and Dad watched on. The neighbour was outside telling the teens to stop, but Mum just laughed and told them to keep going.

One day three of us boys were swimming in the bay behind our house. It was Shaun and our cousin Daniel, who were both eleven, and myself, who was eight. There were no adults.

The two older boys challenged me to a competition to see who could hit the neighbour's boat with mud the most times. The wooden boat was anchored nearby and the neighbour was nowhere in sight. Reaching down into the water, we took up handfuls of mud. Shaun and Daniel were able to hit the boat with ease but I kept missing.

If I had walked away at that point it would have been good, because I hadn't hit the boat at all. The mud on the neighbour's boat had all been put there by Shaun and Daniel. I would have been free from trouble. However, the older boys laughed at me and teased me, and kept laughing and teasing as they made their way out of the water.

I'll show you' I thought as I watched them walk up the bank and out of sight, leaving me alone.

I waited until the tide had gone out further and the boat was slumped over on its side, high and dry. Then, taking my time, I walked around the boat and systematically covered it entirely in mud. It took me a while, but if anything I was a persistent kid. Once I had finished I stood back admiring my work. There was not one glimpse of wood to be seen.

'That'll show them,' I said to myself.

I went off and carried on with my day, giving no more thought to the boat.

Later in the afternoon the phone rang. Dad answered. It was the neighbour. The call wasn't long.

'Oi, you boys!' Dad growled, putting the phone down. 'What did you do to the neighbour's boat?'

Shaun and Daniel were quick to act innocent. 'What?' they said.

'It's covered in mud!' Dad answered.

The boys looked at me.

'What?' I said.

We were ordered back to the beach to clean the neighbour's boat.

'What did you do, Timmy?' Daniel queried as we made our way down the bank.

The boys' jaws dropped when they saw the boat covered in mud.

All I could think was, *Yeah, who missed the boat now?*

The two older boys looked at me.

'Man, Timmy,' Shaun tutted.

'You're an egg,' Daniel stated.

It was a long afternoon cleaning that boat.

¤ ¤ ¤

My cousin Greg and I were walking along Ferry Parade one day, heading home after visiting the Herald Island shop. I was ten and my cousin was sixteen.

A middle-aged woman approached us from across the road. It was Mrs Jones, the lady who lived beside the old Post Office.

'Excuse me,' she said.

Greg and I stopped and turned to face her.

Mrs Jones looked directly at me. 'Show me your bum,' she said.

I wasn't sure I had heard her correctly. 'Eh?' I queried, looking around.

Mrs Jones crossed her arms. 'Show me your bum,' she said again.

Greg frowned and smiled at the same time, looking at me as if to say, *What's this all about, Tim?*

I shrugged. I could feel my face burning red.

'Show me your bum, please,' Mrs Jones repeated.

'No,' I said, 'I don't want to.'

'Then stop showing your bum to my daughters!' Mrs Jones growled.

Greg laughed.

'It's not funny.' Mrs Jones gestured at me. 'He calls out to my daughters, and when they turn and look he drops his pants and shows them his bum. It's rude.'

Greg tried to stop laughing, but couldn't.

Mrs Jones looked at me. 'Are you going to do it again?' she asked.

'No,' I said.

'Good!' Mrs Jones answered.

She about-faced and walked away.

'Tim, eh!' Greg chuckled.

Mum believed that there were people who looked down on her and our family. Mrs Jones and her husband were some of those people, and Mum was big on retribution. She had instructed me to harass the Joneses, to throw stones on their tin roof and to flash my bottom at their teenage daughters whenever I had the chance. Striving to be a good son, I did as I was told. I knew what would happen to me if I didn't. However, after this encounter with Mrs Jones I never harassed her or her family again.

¤ ¤ ¤

Many of my teachers regarded me as a rotten kid that nothing good would ever come from. This was reflected in my atrocious school reports and in the complaints the teachers made to my parents. For each bad report and complaint I got an extra beating at home. Such beatings never made me any cleverer or able to do any better at school. In fact the fear and anxiety because of those beatings only made it worse.

At school I stood out like a sore thumb. I frequently had long periods away, and on returning I had to start all over again and re-establish relationships with my teachers and the children in my class.

I was behind in every subject. I was withdrawn and socially awkward. I smelt of urine because I wet my bed up to the age of ten, and I sometimes wore Dad's long-sleeved button-up shirts to school because I didn't have anything else to wear. I was teased for being poor and dumb, and excluded for being different.

When children weren't calling me Four Eyes, because of my glasses they would chant, 'Tim, Tim, the rubbish bin.' This was because I would scavenge through the school bins in search of food that other kids had chucked away and then eat their leftover pies and cakes. I remember bringing lunch from home, but it was never enough.

I became a showpiece known for head-butting concrete walls and steel bars. I had only done it in front of a couple of kids to begin with to warn them that I was unpredictable and they shouldn't pick on me. However those kids went and told others, and then everyone wanted to see me do it.

¤ ¤ ¤

The dental clinic at school was known as the Murder House and the House of Horrors. It was a place of pain and fear.

I was eight and due for a visit. Once I was lying back in the chair, eyeing the tools of torture, the dental nurse informed me that the teachers had spoken to her about me.

The word was out that I had been stealing.

'Are you a thief, Timothy?' the dental nurse asked, holding up a large needle and syringe in front of my face. 'No one likes a thief, Timothy.'

She leaned over me and held my head firmly as she inserted the needle into my mouth. Now that was scary.

To be fair I had taken some things, but if I'd taken everything I'd been accused of taking I would have filled up my house.

Stealing was in the family. Shaun had been caught doing it only a couple of years before me, and all three of us kids had witnessed Mum getting into trouble for shop lifting. I remember having to sit for ages upstairs in the office of the Smith & Caughey's department store on Queen Street because Mum was being held in the manager's office. Shaun remembers an incident when Mum hit the hat off a policeman as he was trying to arrest her for stealing, and Katie remembers having to wait at the police station while Mum and her mate got processed.

Mum was an opportunist, grabbing the moment whenever it presented itself. When we went to restaurants she sometimes took a fancy to the cutlery and into her bag it would go. Dad never liked it. He would tell her to stop, but Mum didn't listen to Dad. Instead she would complain to the waitress that there was no cutlery. Confused and embarrassed, the poor waitress would apologise and go and get more.

To be fair Mum wasn't the only one. Some of her more wealthy white relatives were into insurance fraud. Mum and Dad tried that. Parked their old car just up the road from Puatahi Marae on the Kaipara and left the keys in it. Ignorant in their racism, they thought some Māori would steal it and then they could claim the insurance.

Problem was, when they went back a week later the car was still sitting there, keys and all.

¤ ¤ ¤

Mum hated people thinking that we were the poor 'Tippanees' and looking down on us. It brought out a a sense of entitlement in her. She felt she had a God-given right to take and do whatever she wanted, and woe to anyone who got in her way. There were many times that us kids had to stand back, embarrassed, as Mum bullied a shop assistant or office clerk for not treating her the way she believed they should. Mum could bring people to tears. Being a white woman allowed Mum to get away with it. It would never have worked for Dad. People, especially some of our white relatives, always racially profiled Dad as a caricature of black US comedians such as *Richard Pryor and Eddie Murphy,* and New Zealand's own *Billy T James.* To them Dad was the Bro. That was until he got ugly and then he was the violent Māori perpetrator.

I was always proud of my Dad, and the racism he experienced affected all of us—some more than others. I would get a beating from him after he'd been singled out and discriminated against.

I think in some ways he was trying to beat and exorcise the Māori out of the both of us. That part of him that was never accepted by the white world he so desperately wanted to be a part of.

The trait of defiance in Mum proved to have a positive side. Her attitude of, '*I'll show you*', drove her to leave her job at the takeaway bar and pursue a long career in banking leading all the way to management. Mum was a badass, a real go getter. She pushed Dad and together they took us out of poverty. Mum's fight and drive is something I respect and admire her for, and I'm thankful because without that learned determination I wouldn't have gone on to succeed later in my own life.

At school I didn't steal out of any sense of entitlement. I just wanted what other kids had.

Kids would bring their cool toys to school and show off. I only had a few toys as a kid and they were mostly second-hand, including some small plastic soldiers that I had bought bags of for 50 cents at a school gala. So I stole a couple of the toys from kids in my class and got a reputation as a thief. Fact is, though, the accusation of me being a thief had come long before I ever took anything.

A week or so after the dentist's interrogation there was an incident with a soccer ball. The teacher walked into the classroom following lunch and firmly proclaimed that a crime had been committed.

She asked for a couple of boys to accompany her to the cloak bay where our bags were stored. As I watched them walk from the classroom I started thinking that this was probably going to lead back to me. However, reflecting on the last few hours, I couldn't think of anything I'd done that I could be in trouble for.

Sure enough, though, I was soon called out to the cloak bay. I found my teacher standing beside a boy who had obviously been crying. My teacher was angry, and at the same time looking triumphant, as if she had finally caught me.

'Is this your schoolbag?' she asked, pointing.

I eyed what looked like my bag, but it couldn't have been because there was a soccer ball stuffed in it. I didn't own a soccer ball. I was excited at seeing one in my bag though. Any kid who owned a ball at school was popular.

'Whose ball is that in your bag, Timothy?' the teacher growled. 'That's Michael's ball, isn't it?'

I had no idea whose ball it was.

'You stole Michael's ball, didn't you, Timothy?' the teacher continued.

All this time I hadn't said a word. I was mystified as to what was going on. Then another boy walked into the cloak bay.

'Yes?' the teacher queried, obviously wondering why he'd left the classroom.

'Uh, we took Michael's ball, Miss,' the boy said. 'We played with it during morning tea.'

'Then how did it get into Timothy's bag?' the teacher asked, looking angrily back at me.

'I thought it was Michael's bag,' the boy said. 'I put it in there after the bell had gone.'

The teacher did not look happy. 'Go back to class, Timothy,' she said, taking the ball from my bag.

My hopes of having just scored a soccer ball were suddenly dashed.

Ever since Mrs Cornelius first arrived at my school she'd been openly hostile towards me, telling me I was a bad kid who needed a firm hand. I knew Mrs Cornelius had big plans for me and her ruler that she hit kids with.

One day there was a school trip and the students who didn't get to go were divided up into different classes for the day. I ended up being placed in Mrs Cornelius's class. Knowing full well the threat I was under, I kept my head down and stayed quiet. However Shaun's mate Stephen and two other senior boys near me played up, and after ignoring Mrs Cornelius's previous warnings the boys were told to come up to the front of the class.

As Stephen and the other two boys made their way to the front Mrs Cornelius produced her ruler. Then she looked at me. 'C'mon, Timothy,' she growled. 'Up you come. You were a part of this too.'

I froze. Everyone looked at me.

'He wasn't part of it, Miss,' Stephen said.

'It didn't look like that to me.' Mrs Cornelius' glare was fixed on me. 'Come on. It won't do you any good to keep me waiting.'

The other two senior boys spoke up on my behalf, telling the teacher that I hadn't been involved.

Mrs Cornelius's eyes narrowed. I could see she was vexed by the fact that I wasn't standing in front of her with my hand held out. Each one of the three boys received a walloping on the hand from Mrs Cornelius' ruler.

When I ended up in Mrs Cornelius' class for my last year at Whenuapai Primary I knew it was only a matter of time before she got me with her ruler. On the first day of the first term she looked at me, and in front of the class said in her stern voice, 'Timothy, I did not want you in my class. I just want you to know that.'

I remember looking around at the other students and thinking, *This is going to be a good year.*

DREAMING FOR KIDNAP

'What are you crying for?' Dad growled from the head of the table.

'I'm not,' I replied.

'You will be,' he said.

Mum and my siblings laughed.

I hadn't done anything wrong. Dad just thought of himself as a bit of a comedian. I never found it funny. I was the only one in our family that Dad talked to like this, and when it came to threats towards me he wasn't kidding.

'I'll put you through the fuckin wall!' was another one of his lines for me.

Mum, Shaun and Katie found this amusing too.

'How are you going to put him through the wall?' Shaun taunted one day.

Dad just laughed.

I was petrified of both of my parents. I flinched whenever they were near. They both took great delight in being sadistic towards me.

Dad's idea of teaching me how to swim was to throw me into the deep end of a public pool. Mum laughed as I thrashed about, struggling to keep my head above the surface. Some nice woman grabbed me and led me to the side, advising me to stick to the shallow end.

To stop me from wetting the bed, Dad would rub my face into the wet patch so hard my nose would bleed. I would then get a hiding for putting blood on the sheets. It didn't stop my bedwetting. The more frightened and traumatised I was the more I wet the bed.

Dad liked to stand over me and order me around, like when I did the dishes. If I hadn't cleaned a plate properly I got whacked. Sometimes I would be so scared with him standing over me I would wet myself. That would trigger another hiding.

Dad would come into my bedroom at night. Sometimes he would upturn my mattress, throwing me out onto the floor. He would wait until I emerged from under the mattress so I could see him laughing at me as he walked away.

I would wrestle my mattress back on to the bed, all the time wondering what was the point of tipping me out. It just seemed to be such a waste of time and effort on Dad's part.

I only had a few toys as a kid and Dad would often dispose of them when I was at school. I would come home and they were simply gone. When I was older he even got rid of my dog which my girlfiend Jo had gifted to me. I had named the dog after my friend, Vincent. To this day I still don't know where that dog ended up. I only hope he had a good life.

Mum was no different towards me. She had the family treat me as though I was a foreign entity, an outsider. It's the only way my siblings have ever known how to treat me.

There were many nights when I had to sleep in Mum's bed as a child and as a teenager. Not because Mum wanted to be close to me, but because Dad was working night shift and Mum found nights challenging and was too scared to sleep alone. There was constant fear and threat around my parents. Doors were always locked and furniture was pushed in front of them. Phone calls would go unanswered, strangers were often hanging around, and police would visit and ask questions.

I have no idea who my parents were afraid of, or who they had wronged, but it was clear at times that someone was upset with them. One morning when I was ten we came out of the house to go somewhere and ended up going nowhere because the lug nuts had been removed from every wheel on the car. It was a good thing Dad had noticed the nuts missing, otherwise we would have had an accident when the wheels came off.

¤ ¤ ¤

I hated spending the night in Mum's bed. She and Dad had a waterbed and the slightest movement would send waves through the mattress making everything rise and fall. Mum would go ballistic, yelling and hitting out whenever I moved because the waves disturbed her sleep. So I would lie awake all night, tensed up like a log, too scared to sleep in case I unconsciously moved and woke Mum.

Whenever there was any sound in the house Mum would send me out in the dark to investigate. Even as a small boy. Shaun and Katie would huddle up with Mum on the couch or in bed as I was sent to look through the house.

Mum would get angry if she turned up in the early hours of the morning and the gate was shut. She would sit in her car at the end of the long driveway with her hand on the horn. The blaring sound would wake everyone, but no one in the house would budge. They all knew whose job it was. I would get out of bed, go outside in the dark and rain, and run down the driveway to open the gate for Mum. Not even the dogs would brave the weather to come out with me. Mum would be yelling and cursing at me from behind the steering wheel for making her wait too long. By the time I had shut the gate and run back up the drive Mum was already inside and in her bedroom with the door closed. There was no 'Goodnight' or 'Thank you'.

Not only was I a security guard and gatekeeper for Mum, I was also her enforcer. If anyone offended her then she would have me get into the car with her late at night and we would go for a drive. Mum would take me to some address and have me smash the letterbox, vehicle or some other item with a baseball bat, and then she would have me urinate on it to finish off. Mum would direct my every move from behind the steering wheel.

At times police and other official looking people would come to the house. Mum would have me stand beside her to face them. She would instruct me to look tough, to be staunch.

'Don't smile,' she'd say. 'And don't say anything—don't even say hello.'

However the officers were always friendly towards me, and when they smiled and said hello I couldn't help but say hello back.

I wasn't allowed to help myself to anything in the house, especially food. If there was fruit in the bowl or bread in the pantry I couldn't take any, and I wasn't allowed to ask for it. Dad would even count the fruit in the bowl and the slices of bread in the bag. I was hungry a lot as a child and as a teenager, but it wasn't because there wasn't food. There was food. I just wasn't allowed it. Family and the parents of friends would comment on how skinny I was and make remarks about me being a bottomless pit as I would eat so much when visiting their homes.

As a child I used to dream of being kidnapped. Dream that some couple, desperate for a child, would steal me away from the day-to-day horror that was my life, and raise me as their own.

One summer I thought I had found a way out.

I was eight or nine years old and playing in the waves at Matheson Bay, near Leigh, north of Auckland. Some teenagers lost control of a catamaran and ran me down in the surf. I ended up pinned under the cat. I gasped for air and struggled to keep my head above water. Adults up on the beach noticed and rushed to my aid. They carried me up onto the shore and laid me out on the grass. A crowd formed around me. Two adults were kneeling, looking me over, trying to ascertain if I had any serious injuries. Turning my head to the side, I could see my parents watching from where they sat with Uncle Todd further down the beach.

The woman kneeling over me spoke of taking me to hospital. I wanted to go—I wanted to be seriously injured so I could go with her and never come back. I was thinking that this was it, I had found my escape.

A feeling of despair came over me as I watched Dad get to his feet and walk in my direction. I looked at the woman. I just wanted her to pick me up and whisk me away. Inside I was screaming to be rescued.

Without saying a word, Dad pushed through the small crowd. Bending down, he grabbed me by my hair with one hand and wrenched me up from the ground, throwing me over his shoulder. Horror filled the faces of those who had been trying to help me. Some tried to say something, but Dad was in staunch mode which was intimidating for anyone.

Dad carried me down the beach and dropped me on the ground behind Mum and Uncle Todd, who just sat there looking out to sea. Dad sat down next to them.

Mum glared over her shoulder at me. 'You're fine.'

There was no rescue.

If I had been removed from my home chances are I may have ended up in a worst situation. Even within the wider family there were others who were just as abusive and violent as Mum and Dad. What was clear to me as a kid though was that my home was not a safe place and I wanted out. This meant that I would latch on to any available adults, some good, some not so good.

SUCCESSES

I was a delayed reader. One of the scariest things I ever had to do as a small child was to take home readers and try to read them aloud to my parents. It was the same with my spelling and the weekly lists of words that I had to learn how to spell. Mum and Dad got angry with every mistake I made. The more angry they got the more scared I would get and the more I would stutter and make mistakes. I got whacked every time. Thankfully it got to the point where my parents got so fed up they refused to waste any more time on me and my homework. It wouldn't be till the age of 12 that I would read my first chapter book.

However in year 6 I was excited when Book Week arrived. There had been book weeks at school before, but this time it was different—I was different. With Miss Foote for a teacher I was excelling, and starting to believe that anything was possible. My school report that year was the best report I'd ever had. In my previous years it didn't seem to matter how hard I tried, I always failed. Now, with Miss Foote, I was being rewarded for my efforts. I had even won an award for my Kashin the Elephant ASB poster. My entire class, including me, now believed that I was a writer, because Miss Foote had announced I was after I had written her an 'outstanding' story. I had only written it because I was smitten and wanted to marry her. Miss Foote had been so impressed that she had taken me by the hand and led me around to other classrooms so that the students could see my work as an example of good writing. So when it came time for Book Week I was ready to give it my best.

This year for Book Week classes would visit other rooms, and the teachers of those rooms would take them through a craft activity based on story. In one classroom we would make masks, in another room we would have to design a book cover, and in the hall we would have to work in groups and draw huge giants on large pieces of newsprint that had been laid out on the floor.

Those students who demonstrated focus, worked diligently and did well at an activity would be awarded a certificate. The aim was to see how many certificates you could get in the week, with five being the most. One for each day. If you got all five you got a prize.

On Monday I completed the first activity and scored my first certificate.

I was so pleased with myself. I wanted to show Miss Foote, but being in another class all day I never got to see her. Still, I was certain I could get a second certificate. Miss Foote would be impressed with that.

On Tuesday I did it. I earned my second certificate.

Wow, this is cool, I thought.

I was on a high. I was loving the activities, and for once I was leading the pack. I didn't want it to stop. On Wednesday I stuck my head down, got creative and focused on the task at hand, and at the end of the day received my third certificate.

I was on a roll. I was now believing that I could do it—that I could achieve five certificates by the end of the week. I still had no one to share my success with. As I was in someone else's class each day I wasn't seeing Miss Foote at all. My parents certainly weren't interested in my achievements. I got more attention from Mum and Dad for a bad report than I ever did for a good one. Whenever I tried to show Mum a certificate she would sneer at it.

'What, do you want—a medal or something?' she'd say as she walked away.

But succeeding at Book Week had nothing to do with my parents or even the school. Because of Miss Foote I now believed in myself. I had had enough of coming last. For once in my life I was flourishing and I wanted more of it.

I finished Thursday with my fourth certificate. There was no stopping me.

On Friday it was a mask-making class.

Yes, I thought, looking at all the materials in front of me. *I can do this.*

While the majority of the kids didn't know what mask to make I had my idea ready to go. I set to work.

'What are you making?' kids asked me, looking for ideas.

'I don't know,' I said, keeping mine a secret.

A lot of the children were mucking around, playing and talking. The relief teacher warned them that they needed to get working in order to get their masks finished on time. I ignored everyone and focused on making the best mask I could. At the end of the day my Medusa mask inspired by *Clash of the Titans* was finished. I had done it. I had worked well, been quiet and created a masterpiece. I knew I had my fifth certificate.

The teacher walked around the room, inspecting the creations. She announced the masks that had earned a book week certificate. She pointed out mine. Five certificates in five days—I had done it! I couldn't have been happier.

As the teacher approached me with my certificate a girl started to complain. She had been one of the students who'd been mucking around. Normally she was a grade A student and was used to achieving. I had never had an A in my life.

The girl said it was unfair that I was getting another certificate as I had already earned four of them during the week.

The teacher stopped in front of me and listened to the girl's argument.

I knew that the goal of the week was to earn five certificates. It came down to working hard and getting each task completed, and I had done that.

'Okay, fair's fair,' the teacher said, turning away from me. 'I will award the certificate to someone else.' And she did.

The girl smiled at me cruelly.

I was devastated. I looked down at my mask. The teacher had already acknowledged my mask as a winner. I had made sure I'd done everything right. I had followed the rules. I had focused on my work, I hadn't interrupted anyone and I had finished on time.

How could another student have this much power? The power to decide whether I got my fifth certificate or not? How could the world be so unfair?

It was another failure on an increasingly long list of failures. The four certificates suddenly meant nothing. There was no way I was going to show

Miss Foote now. Any confidence I had gained over the week fell away, along with any faith in fairness in the world.

I had learnt that just because you work hard doesn't guarantee that you'll succeed.

¤ ¤ ¤

The next year I decided to put some effort into cross country. After having experienced some successes under the guidance and support of Miss Foote, and now having the compassion and understanding of Mrs Battersby, I was feeling that anything was possible. In the classroom I'd had to do some reading on running as part of a classroom project in the lead-up to the 1984 Olympics. There had also been time to practise running at school and around Herald Island. I figured that if I went in with the same attitude I'd had with Book Week the year before I could do quite well.

On the day of the cross country boys were spouting off about where they were going to come. Many were convinced they were going to be first. One asked me where I thought I was going to place.

'I'm going for third,' I said, not wanting to aim too high.

The boys laughed at me.

'Yeah, third from the back, you mean,' one jeered.

'There's no way you're going to come third,' another added.

It didn't matter what they said. In my mind I had it set that I was going to take third place.

That afternoon us boys were all bunched up on the starting line. I could see that I was going to have to break out ahead of the group. I was determined not to get left behind. The starting signal sounded and we were off. I ran out for the front, not wanting to lose the leading pack. I ran hard, then realised there was no leading pack. It was just me. I was certain the fast boys must be hot on my tail, those boys who'd been spouting off before the race and who were renowned in the school for their running. They were even revered by many of the teachers for their racing prowess.

But no, I was on my own. I was leading the way. I couldn't believe it. I was coming first.

I wanted to look behind me, but I remembered what I had read about long distance running, and kept my focus forward on the couple of meters of ground just ahead of me, kept my pace steady, and made sure I didn't over exert myself.

The race was three laps and I led for the 1st and 2nd. All the way around I was expecting to be passed by those boys.

Two passed me on the last lap. That was no surprise. I even told myself it was okay because they were faster than me. They were the ones the teachers believed in.

However I had said that I was going to come third, so nobody else was getting past me. And with that thought I did it. I came third. Much to the surprise of the staff and students.

As I bent over and fought to catch my breath I was amazed at what I had achieved. However a question came to mind. Why had I limited myself to third place?

I realised I had been close to winning. I had been coming first. I could have won. I had said that I would come in third place, and I did. What would have happened if I'd said I was going to come first?

Where did the belief that these boys were faster than me come from? It came from the school, the teachers, the students, my peers—even from myself. Many said that I wouldn't and couldn't come third, yet I had proved them wrong.

I realised that I had the power to change things for myself. Just because others placed limitations on me didn't mean I had to accept those limitations. When it came to who I was and what I could achieve, no parent, teacher, adult, child, or myself should limit me. I did not have to consent to the beliefs of others. I did not have to be a failure and a loser just because others saw me that way. In the cross country I had smashed through what others had thought of me.

I could now see that there was a lot more smashing to be done.

HERBIE AND PRINCESS

My childhood was blessed with animals. We had lots of cats and dogs when I was growing up.

One little dog was called Herbie. Mum named him after Disney's Volkswagen Beetle car. Half dachshund and half chihuahua, he was black in colour with a patch of white on his chest. He would howl along with the midday siren that sounded every day from the Herald Island Fire Station.

Herbie was my faithful companion throughout my childhood. I confided in Herbie, venting to him about everything that was going on at home and at school. That little dog would just sit there, looking straight up at me and take in my every word. He was the best listener.

Herbie would be running along beside me on all my adventures. There were various people that the two of us would visit on Herald Island. Usually elderly people who were living alone. I would sit and talk with them, and they would give Herbie and me biscuits and tell us stories. I would have to keep an eye on Herbie though—he wasn't a well-mannered guest. He would cock his leg and pee on the old person's furniture. Especially if they had cats.

When it came to dogs Dad and I had a connection. He loved them as much as I did.

Herbie was not a contained dog. He was left free to roam the neighbourhood. One afternoon he ran in the path of a car on the road outside our house and got hit. He gave an almighty yelp and took off. Dad sent me to find him. I knew exactly where Herbie would be. I went down behind our house where the bank was covered in bush, to an area Herbie and I often mucked about in.

I had a certain way of calling him that he always responded to.

'Heeeeeerbie!' I cried. 'Heeeeeerbie!'

I knew he would come to me. Herbie trusted me. I was safe. But I was frightened, and worried that he was badly hurt.

Herbie limped out of the undergrowth. He was bleeding from the pit of his left hind leg. I picked him up gently in my arms, getting blood all over my top, and carried him up to the house.

Dad drove us to the Kumeū vet. Herbie was taken straight into the operating room and they set to work on him. The vet was oblivious to the fact that a small boy had followed them. I cried at the sight of them working on my little dog, on my best friend. Dad noticed and stepped in front of me, blocking my view so I couldn't see.

Dad was angry through the whole ordeal, especially afterwards when Herbie would whimper in pain at night during his recovery. 'Shut up, ya bloody mutt!' he'd yell.

However, for that brief moment in the vets Dad had shielded me from seeing Herbie suffering, and I appreciated that.

¤ ¤ ¤

Princess was Dad's dog. She was a German Shepherd—a beautiful-natured dog who mothered us kids, and she was a very protective mother. When we swam in the bay behind our house Princess would paddle ahead and round us up, refusing to let us go out too far. When we walked Princess on a lead around Herald Island she wouldn't let us go near adults, even when we knew them. She would drag us away from them, or get in between us and them, and push us back.

Princess was a loving dog and Dad adored her. However not even Princess was safe from Dad's rage. Dad took out his anger on the dogs just as he did with me. I think that's why the dogs and I had such an affinity with one another.

When Princess got off her lead, ran up onto the porch and pushed the cats out of the way to eat their food, Dad got her in the corner and kicked her repeatedly with his boots on. The whole neighbourhood would have heard Princess yelping. Other times Dad took to her with a piece of wood.

Princess got cancer when she was ten. I was scared because Mum had only just beaten cancer herself, and had lost one of her friends to it at the same time. Cancer had taken a few people we'd known, so I knew how bad it could be. Princess spent a lot of time at the vets, eventually going in for an operation. All that day I mucked around in my room, anxiously waiting to hear how Princess was.

When the phone rang in the afternoon Mum was at work so Dad answered it. He spoke solemnly. I waited in my bedroom, trying to glean as much information as I could from what Dad was saying. Katie and Shaun were elsewhere in the house, doing their own thing.

Dad soon hung up.

I waited.

'Timmy,' Dad called.

Frightened, I walked out of my bedroom and approached him. He was sitting on the floor in front of the coffee table where the phone sat.

Dad looked up at me. 'She's gone, boy,' he said. 'Princess is gone. She died on the operating table.'

I burst into tears. I had lost a mother.

Dad opened his arms to me. I collapsed into him and together we cried.

This is the one tender moment that I had with Dad—in fact the only tender moment I ever had with either of my parents. Here Dad needed me and we comforted each other. He would never let me in again.

That afternoon Paul Young was singing on the radio 'Every time you go away, you take a piece of me with you'. From that day on I cried whenever I heard that song, thinking of Princess.

¤ ¤ ¤

One night I woke suddenly and sat straight up, knowing that something was wrong with my little dog, Herbie. I couldn't explain it, but I knew he was hurt. I was in my early teens and staying up at Uncle Todd's bach at Leigh. The rest of the house was asleep. I knew I wasn't going to be able to do anything until the morning, so. I lay back down and just hoped Herbie was okay.

In the morning I told my cousin that I'd had a bad feeling about my dog. She let me use the phone to call home.

Mum answered.

'Is Herbie there?' I asked. 'I'm worried about him.'

'Yes, yes,' Mum said. 'Herbie's fine. You don't need to come back. You just stay up there until the holidays have finished.'

Mum was always dumping me on other people. My siblings and I spent every Christmas holiday's at Uncle Todd's bach at Leigh. While I appreciated my Uncle's hospitality, I didn't always feel welcome. I would spend a lot of the holiday on my own doing my own thing.

When I hung up the phone I knew something wasn't right. Mum wasn't one for telling the truth. Stuck at Leigh and powerless to do anything about it, I went about my days. However Herbie never left my mind. I felt that he had needed me and that I hadn't been there.

Herbie and I had a long history together. I was the one Herbie came to after he'd been hit by the car. I was the one who had carried him home, getting blood all over me and I did that again after he was savaged by a much larger dog. In return Herbie had gotten me through the abuse and violence of my childhood. I didn't want to imagine a world without him.

When my cousins finally dropped me home at the end of the holidays the first thing I asked was, 'Where is Herbie?'

'He's around,' Mum said. 'I just saw him this morning.'

I didn't believe her. I went outside and looked for him. 'Heeeeeerbie!,' I called.

Mum came out, glaring. She didn't want me making a scene in front of my cousins. 'He's fine!

From Mum's reaction I knew something was wrong.

When my cousins had left Mum told me that Herbie had gone missing. She hadn't wanted to tell me because she didn't want me coming home early.

I went out and scoured the neighbourhood, but I didn't find anything.

'Heeeeeerbie!' I called throughout the day.

We had moved from Herald Island and had been living in Makarau for a few years by this stage. Herbie was old and blind, but he still knew his way home. I hoped he was out there somewhere, still okay. Yet I couldn't shake the feeling that my friend had gone.

A couple of months later, on the bus going home from high school, a mate started laughing.

'My dad shot your dog,' he said.

'What?' I frowned.

'You know, your little black dog,' the mate smiled. 'Dad shot him.'

'Why?' I asked.

'For fun,' the boy answered. 'Dad was drunk one night. He used your dog for target practice.'

I knew that would have been when I woke up at Leigh.

'You should have heard your dog yelping.' The boy laughed.

I wanted to hit the boy, I wanted to shut him up. He was supposed to be my mate. He'd been around me for two months knowing that his dad had killed Herbie, and he was only telling me now.

The boy had timed it perfectly, telling me just as the bus was pulling up at his stop. It left me little time to respond. I wasn't sure if it was right to let the boy get off the bus without beating him to a pulp, but I let him go. As much as I wanted revenge, there was nothing I could do that would bring Herbie back. I was angry, yet mostly what I felt was hurt and betrayal by my friend and his family. Yet I was also grateful to my friend for having told me. I believe he did so out of loyalty. I'm sure his family would have told him to keep his mouth shut.

Herbie had been a special friend to me. He helped me to get through. He was a great listener and loyal. I was blessed to have him in my life for as long as I did, and the love that he gave me still remains. Thank you, Herbie.

¤ ¤ ¤

When visitors came to our house Mum would give them the grand tour, showing off her collection of animals and saying how much each one had cost. Mum would also talk of the personal sacrifice and effort she had put into each of the animal's individual care. In reality, though, Mum was quick to get bored with each animal because she constantly found something new to focus on. She always started out with the best of intentions, however she had to keep moving in order to avoid the trauma of her past. Mum's animals would then be forgotten and neglected. Many of them met sad ends due to the lack of care. For example, after I left home Mum's horses and pet cow died of thirst because Mum hadn't given them access to water.

One of Mum's prized animals was a dog called Jonathon, who was a pedigree English Mastiff. Mum would boast that she had paid almost two thousand dollars for him. One Saturday morning Mum had me help her with Jonathon. She wanted to get the dog out of the house and into the garage. Jonathon didn't want to go. Mum had the dog by the collar and was pulling from the front while I pushed him from the rear. The large, heavy dog sat back with all his weight, refusing to budge. The collar slipped off Jonathon's head, causing Mum to fall back. In a fit of rage Mum got up and lashed out with the collar—not at her prized dog, but at me. She whipped me across the head with it and I was cut by the buckle.

Once Jonathon was in the garage Mum wanted to see my wound. She was concerned at the sight of blood. I was 14 and fed up with being mistreated. I knew she only wanted to see it so she could downplay her actions and dismiss the wound as nothing. It was a tactic she had used many times before.

Refusing to let her see the cut, I walked away, retreating to my bedroom, and avoided her for the rest of the day.

The next morning Mum wanted a Sunday family lunch. Mum and Dad were hardly ever home. They were always out separately, doing their own thing. Sometimes us kids wouldn't see our parents for days. Then there would be times like this, where Mum would turn up and demand that everyone behaved like a family.

Mum cooked a meal and had everyone sit around the table. The food was dished out.

I sat in my usual spot. Mum and Dad had always made me sit at the end of the table away from them. Shaun's place was beside Dad and Katie's next to Mum.

We were ready to eat when Mum stood up abruptly, garnering our attention. We watched her march out of the lounge and down the hallway like a sulky teen.

'What's wrong, Mum?' Katie called out.

There was no reply.

Mum disappeared into her bedroom.

Dad got up and went after her. I started to eat—I had learnt from a young age not to muck around when it came to food because I never knew where the next meal was coming from.

Shortly afterwards Dad returned to the table. It was then Katie's turn to go down the hallway and console Mum. When Katie came back Shaun dutifully headed off to Mum's bedroom. After he returned I kept on eating. I had never been included in consoling Mum before, so I figured my participation wasn't required.

Dad, Shaun and Katie all glared at me.

'Man, Timmy,' Katie sneered.

'You're so selfish,' Shaun tutted.

'You better get your arse in there, boy!' Dad threatened.

I got up from the table and walked through the house. I had a good idea what Mum was after. She would be wanting me to take responsibility for her actions the day before.

'Mum,' I said.

She turned away, refusing to look at me. Instead she attended her face in the mirror.

I apologised for the incident with Jonathon the dog, for the collar having come off, for her having to hit me, for my head bleeding, and I said sorry for having walked away.

Mum sent me back to the table without a glance.

Not long afterwards she followed—recovered, refreshed and renewed. She took her seat at the dining table and laughed and chatted with the others as though nothing had happened.

Mum was never one to take responsibility.

OMAHA

One day in summer a large group of us converged onto Omaha Beach for some fun in the sun and surf. My siblings and I were staying at my Uncle Todd's bach at Leigh for the Christmas holidays, and Mum and Dad had decided to stay a couple of days.

As soon as we got to Omaha our group disbanded, with people going off in all directions. I joined others splashing about in the waves. Sometime later I realised I was on my own amongst the bathers with no family members in sight. This wasn't unusual though so I didn't think anything of it, and carried on playing in the water.

Soon I found that I was in trouble. I had gone off to the side and become caught in a rip. I started being pulled out to sea. There were people around, adults and children, but I didn't call for help. My parents had taught me to keep my mouth shut and not to make a fuss or cause trouble. My mere existence seemed to be an inconvenience for everybody so I could only watch the people grow smaller as I was pulled away.

At first I fought against the rip. I thrashed about and swam hard, but it didn't get me anywhere. I just got tired fast, and my arms and legs started to cramp up. It was difficult trying to stay above the waves and I was having to spit out mouthfuls of salt water and while gasping for air.

At the top of each wave I could see the beach, but it would disappear when the wave passed. Land was getting further and further away. The rip turned, taking me north. It was quiet out this far. The noises from the beach had faded. No one would hear me if I yelled now.

There was no pretending out here. There was only reality. I knew that no one was coming for me. It would be ages before anyone would notice that I was missing. I was scared and on my own. I looked up at the clouds, the blue sky and the sun. It was a beautiful day.

'It's not looking good, God,' I said.

I had felt panic the whole time, yet I refused to let it take over. Even though I hadn't actually joined a martial arts school at this stage I had watched movies and television programmes. I considered myself a martial artist and a master of my body. I controlled my breathing, and worked to settle my heartbeat which had been racing. I softened my body and told myself to stay calm. The strong current had already shown me that if I fought against it I was going to lose. I could doggy paddle, but anything more than that and the cramp I was feeling in my legs and arms got worse.

'Please God,' I said, 'I don't want to die.'

I was managing to keep myself afloat so I started to think of what I should do. I remembered rips being talked about at school. Calm spots on the beach that we should avoid because it was a channel within the water that would drag you out to sea. I decided to go with the current and to doggy paddle my way towards the edge of it in the hope that I could break free, and come out the side.

I had swallowed so much sea water that I felt as though I was going to vomit. My arms and my legs were aching.

'Keep going, Tim,' I told myself. 'Just keep going. Slow and steady.'

It was the school cross county all over again.

I constantly moved my arms and legs until eventually I found I was no longer being pulled. I had done it. I had come out the side of the rip. But I wasn't safe yet.

I was some distance out from shore, and my arms and legs were heavy. I knew there was no time for resting or for giving up. I could see the northern point of Omaha.

'Keep going,' I told myself, paddling slowly through the water. 'You can do this—you can reach the shore. You'll be able to rest when you're on the beach.'

The waves kept coming. Up and down I went. In the back of my mind I started hearing the music for *Jaws* and thinking that a shark was about to grab and pull me under to the depths below. I used that fear to keep me moving forward.

I told myself over and over again that I could do it, that I could reach land. I continued to control my breathing and keep my body calm. I ached all over. As I drew nearer to the shore I fought the urge to rush, the urge to allow the panic and fear to take over. I thought about the story of the tortoise and the hare. The methodical strategy of the tortoise would win this race. I knew I had to conserve my energy; otherwise I wouldn't make it.

I plodded on. It seemed to take forever. Now and then I would lower my legs in the hope that my feet would find the bottom—that it would be shallow enough for me to stand. But it never was.

In between the rising waves my eyes were fixed firmly on the beach. Soon I noticed two people walking along the sand. It was hard to make them out at first, but as I drew closer I thought it might be Mum and Dad.

I kept paddling and inching my way forward. Soon I was close enough to see that it was my parents. They walked up to meet the sea, looking out through the choppy water at me.

'Where the hell have you been?' Mum yelled. 'Everyone's waiting to go! You'll be bloody left behind if you don't hurry up!'

And with that she and Dad turned and walked away, heading back down the beach towards the main carpark.

I watched them go as I trudged on, hoping to reach land. I wasn't sure if Mum was angry at me because she'd had to wait for me to turn up, or because I had turned up at all.

In a little while my feet found the sandy bottom. I could stand. I had made it.

My arms and legs felt as though they had given up completely now. They were cramped up tight. All I wanted to do was collapse on the beach for a while to catch my breath. However the threat of having to face Mum's fury meant I had to keep going. I now had a long walk ahead of me.

My body was hurting as I walked along the shore. I was relieved to be back on land though, relieved to be alive. I had been so close to drowning, but I had saved myself.

At home I had been living a fantasy, refusing to see the reality. I had been pretending that Mum and Dad loved me and that everything was okay. I wanted to believe I lived a normal life with a good family, like all those ones I had seen on TV.

However out there in the sea, in the midst of my near-death experience, the charade had crumbled. No amount of pretending or wishful thinking had been going to save me. No one had been coming to rescue me. I had been forced to accept the reality of my situation and deal with it. I had had to turn inwards, to myself. It had been up to me to get myself to shore—to save myself. And that's exactly what I did.

This was the day that I woke up. From that point on the blinders were off. I would never look at Mum, Dad and my family the same ever again. It was a turning point in my life.

There would be no more pretending and playing happy families. From now on I would be real. It was up to me to get to where I wanted to be in life.

No one paid me any attention when I reached the car park. No one noticed how exhausted I was. I didn't tell any of my family about my ordeal. In fact, I didn't tell anyone. I didn't want to make a fuss.

GETTING TO DO KARATE

At 11 I fell in love with martial arts. Whenever I found anyone who had studied it I would get them to show me everything they knew. I copied moves from films and looked at martial arts books whenever I had the chance. I practised for a year by myself before I ever got to step into a martial arts school, and it took some strategising to get there.

When I was 12 some of the kids at my new school were doing karate. I wanted to join, but I knew that if I asked Mum and Dad they would say 'No'.

That wasn't the case with Katie though. Typically Katie got to do whatever she wanted. She managed to get away with a lot too, though it was more neglect than being spoilt.

Dad was a heavy sleeper and he snored loudly. He worked shift work, and because of this he would sleep all hours of the day. Living on Herald Island we were close to the Whenuapai Air Force Base, and every now and then the base would put on air shows where planes and fighter jets would fly around demonstrating manoeuvres. Shaun and I would be up on the roof of our house, watching the jets shoot pass and covering our ears for the thundering roar of the engines that followed. In between the sound of the jets and the mock bombs going off at the base the two of us boys could hear Dad snoring from inside the house. There wasn't much that could wake Dad.

Katie learned how to use this to her advantage.

'Hey Dad?' she'd say, shaking him as he slept in bed. 'Dad?'

'Mm,' he would murmur.

'We're going up the road,' Katie would say. 'Is that okay?'

There was no reply.

I'd be in the lounge, listening and waiting for Katie to work her magic.

'Dad?' Katie shook him again. 'Is that okay?'

'Mm,' Dad groaned.

'That's good enough,' Katie smiled.

And off we went. My sister and I were known for wandering the streets of Herald Island.

When we arrived home later in the evening Dad would be up and out of bed. 'Where were you fellas?' he would growl.

'We were up the road!' Katie growled back.

'Who said you could go up there?'

'You did,' Katie replied defiantly.

'Eh?' Dad said, looking baffled.

'I asked you when you were asleep,' Katie explained. 'You said yes.'

'I don't remember that,' Dad grumbled.

'Well you said it,' Katie stated.

Dad would go back to doing whatever he was doing and nothing more was said.

It worked every time.

So when it came to wanting to do karate I knew that if Katie wanted to do it as well I'd have a chance.

I went up to her. 'Hey, Katie?' I said. 'Do you want to do karate? C'mon, it'll be fun.'

She gave it some thought. 'Uh, yeah,' she nodded.

'You ask Mum then,' I said.

Katie found Mum in her room. 'Hey, Mum,' she said, 'I want to do karate.'

'Okay,' Mum replied. 'But your brother will have to do it with you.'

Yes! I was in.

Katie and I started karate lessons at the Dairy Flat Hall. Shaun was happy to take us because it meant he got to drive. He had recently passed his driving license and Mum had got him a car. It was an old Datsun and Shaun, the wannabe rally driver, was grabbing every opportunity to get out on the road.

He and I had even become Dad's roadside assistance team. In the early hours of the morning the phone would ring and it would be Dad calling from someone's house to say he'd come off the road again. Mum was never home, so Shaun and I would get into the Datsun and go looking for him. We always took rope, which we'd use to pull Dad's car out of some ditch. On getting free, Dad would get back behind the steering wheel.

'You shouldn't be driving, Dad,' Shaun would say. 'You're drunk.'

'I'm fine,' Dad would slur. 'My car knows the way home.'

And off he would go to some other party. Shaun and I never liked it. We were always worried Dad would end up killing someone on the road.

The main reason Shaun was keen to take Katie and I to Karate was because he got to pick up his girlfriend on the way.

Our karate teacher was Sensei Peter Lee, a white man from Auckland's North Shore. He had adopted the name Lee for marketing purposes.

Peter taught us a combination of Shotokan Karate, Judo and Okinawa Kobudo—weaponry training. He called the combination Go Shintai Kai Karate. He said it meant 'a place of honour'.

The class was once a week, but I trained every day at home. I was relentless, practising the techniques over and over again. I didn't have any money so anything I needed for my training I had to make myself.

For a punching bag I hung up a sack of sand from a tree. I would hit it to condition my fists. It wasn't the best thing to do and I wouldn't recommend it. It hurt and took the skin off my knuckles, yet I kept going back to it.

I would go into the bush and gather all sorts of sticks for my training. I found an old chisel and, using the skills that a carver, Sakapo, had taught me when we holidayed with Uncle Todd in Fiji, I carved myself a bokken (a wooden practice sword). I spent many hours out on the lawn just trying to master weapons. Especially the nunchaku, a weapon made famous by the late Bruce Lee. Nunchaku consist of two sticks connected at one end by a short chain or rope. I made my first pair by drilling a hole through the end of two lengths of wood from an old broom handle and then tying them together with a shoe lace. Eventually, though, I managed to get some money from mowing a neighbour's lawn up the road and from selling goods that weren't mine to sell, and brought a proper pair from the Martial Arts store in town.

I was constantly hitting myself with the nunchaku. I hit myself in the head, the funny bone and the groin, and each time I would end up in tears on the ground, clutching my wound. Once the pain and tears had subsided I would get back up and do it all over again, spinning those nunchaku as fast as I could, over and over, until I got it right. I never gave up. I felt strong, fit and confident.

The pressure was on for me to learn as much as I could from Sensei Lee because I knew that eventually Katie's enthusiasm for karate would run out, and once she stopped going I would have to stop too.

In the meantime, though, Katie loved it. She was often the only girl there, and the only person with brown skin. Yet she used karate as an outlet for her aggression, and she liked nothing better than to fight the white boys. While us seniors trained up one end of the hall, my sister and the boys around her age would line up at the other end. There each student would take a turn to step out ahead of the line, and face each of the other students in a one-on-one round of sparring. Katie loved it.

When it was her turn out in front Katie would stand there with her fists at the ready and smile widely at each boy who stood in front of her.

The boys found her grin disconcerting.

'Why is she smiling?' they would say.

When the instructor called, 'Go!' Katie would laugh out loud and charge at her opponent. The boys would run to get away from her.

'I'm not fighting her,' they'd say. 'Something's wrong with her.'

Katie preferred the boys who didn't run—the ones who stayed and faced her. She got to hit them. The more fear the boys showed the more confident Katie got.

Katie is all grown up with her own adult sons now. In the past couple of years her and I have reconnected. Recently I reminded her about her days at karate and how she used to hassle those poor boys. Katie couldn't stop laughing.

¤ ¤ ¤

Martial arts was my thing and it was what I became known for. It also gave me a dream that started when I was in my teens. I dreamed that one day I would become a martial arts instructor with my own school. People talked about how good I was, especially martial arts teachers, so I knew my dream was possible. I spent a lot of time exploring that dream in my head. I could see it and feel it. I imagined having a space that was like a temple where kids like me could learn martial arts and get help to become masters of their lives. The dream kept me going. It kept me planning for the future. When things got bad I would turn to my training and my dream and believe that one day I would be a master of my own school. Believing in a positive future made my life endurable, made each day bearable. I kept telling myself I would get there, that I would reach my dream, and that once I was there my life would be better.

The art I really wanted to learn was ninjutsu—the art of the ninja. I had magazines about it. Ninja posters covered my walls. I watched movies and read comics.

Then in the mid eighties the first ever Togakure-Ryū ninjutsu seminar was held in Auckland. It was hosted by the late Michael Gent and featured Australian Wayne L. Roy, who was a student of Grandmaster Dr Masaaki Hatsumi of Japan. The seminar was packed with men. Mum was happy for me to go as it got rid of me for two whole days. I was one of just a handful of teenagers there. I now had another style to mix with what I had already learnt.

I was so grateful that I got to go. Katie had lost interest in karate by this stage and so I hadn't been able to continue with classes. Thankfully I now knew enough to be able to keep training on my own at home, and a number of kids had got me to hold classes in the gymnasium for them at high school during lunchtime. This meant that I had others to practise against and through teaching I was able to hone my skills even more. My plan was to return to Go Shintai Kai and ninjutsu when I was older and independent from my family.

My drama teacher at high school was impressed by my dedication and success within the martial arts. I failed every test and exam at school, but had passed all of my belt gradings before I had stopped going. The teacher asked me to give a demonstration at an up and coming open evening for parents. It was nice to have people believing I was actually good at something, so I accepted the challenge.

The teacher gave me a written note giving me permission to bring some of my martial arts weapons to school each day so that I could practice for my performance. By this point I had manage to accumulate quite a collection of them.

When I got to school each morning I would leave the weapons in the teacher's office, practice with them when I was in his class, and then pick them up at the end of the day. There was an array of weapons including a steel sword, nunchaku, Kama, Sai and even Shuriken, also known as throwing stars. My teacher trusted me and I didn't let him down. After all I was representing my martial arts school and my instructor, and I took that very seriously.

One interval a group of boys approached me and each in turn proceeded to apologise and shake my hand.

'No hard feelings, eh, Tim,' one said.

I had no idea what the boys were apologising for. Later I found out they had an issue with me, and had planned to fight me, but that all changed when they heard I had brought weapons to school. They were thinking that I was going to go all ninja on them. They had obviously watched too many movies.

My demonstration for the performance night went well, and cemented my reputation as a skilled martial artist.

Mum came to the evening by default as she had to pick me up. She got to see my demonstration. She seemed embarrassed, but she never said anything about it afterwards. My teacher never noticed her there.

HETA AND MARY
Year 8/Form 2

Mum and Dad sold our house on Herald Island. I wasn't happy to be leaving my friends and the people I knew, and I didn't like leaving the island and the Waitematā Harbour. My parents brought a lifestyle block in Makarau, north of Auckland.

On the first day at our new home our new neighbours, Heta and Mary, turned up with some fresh fish to welcome us. They lived up on the hill behind us, sharing a large block of Māori land, a papakainga, with a number of other families.

Heta and Mary lived simply. A large sheet of plywood acted as a back door to their house and many of the windows were broken. There was little in the way of furniture inside, and there was no running water and no electricity. This was common around these parts, with some of my schoolmates and their families living in shacks with dirt floors. Yet Heta and Mary were happy. They were a warm and welcoming older couple that my parents chose to keep a distance from. Mum and Dad were keen to stay away from the Māori style of life. To them it meant poverty and struggle. Over time, though, Katie and I got to know Heta, Mary and their adult son, Alex, well.

Visiting them I would sometimes find an old television set sitting precariously on the edge of a car that had its bonnet up. The TV was wired up to the car battery, and while there wasn't much of a picture on the screen, Heta would listen to the commentary as he pottered around his backyard.

A year or so later, when I finally got to do martial arts Heta would sit on a stump overlooking our house, lean on his walking stick and watch me practise on our lawn. With an audience to impress I had to train harder, so it was a big help.

When Heta got sick I would go up and mow his lawns and deliver food that Mum had made for him and Mary. Mary would get me to go in and sit with Heta as he lay in his hospital bed, which was on loan from the hospital. Heta had come home to die.

Heta liked my company, but as a young teen I didn't know what to say to a dying man, so little was ever said. I just sat there with him.

When Heta passed he was taken to Kakanui Marae. Mary and Alex had me sit up the end with them next to the coffin in the wharenui. Unbeknown to me at the time, some relatives were angry that I was placed so close to the coffin and things were said through mihi. Having been brought up around te reo Māori I recognised a little of what was being said. I could tell that someone was in trouble. I just didn't understand enough to know that it was me.

When Mary told me what was going on I was devastated. I got up to move away, but she grabbed my arm and pulled me back.

'You stay right here, boy,' she said. 'You're not going anywhere. This is your place, here beside my Heta, just as it was when he was sick.'

'Yeah, Tim,' Alex added. 'You stay there, bro, next to Dad.'

Following the tangi, Katie and I stayed close with Mary and Alex. There were nights where I would sit with Mary in front of her potbelly fireplace— the only light in the house. Mary's grand, old, wrinkled face would glow as she ranted and raved, telling me how bad Pākehā were, how she couldn't stand them, couldn't trust them, and how certain ones had wronged her. She kept feeding old beef bones into the fire as she talked.

I was thinking that my white, Pākehā skin must be shining bright. Yet Mary didn't see me as Pākehā. She said I was more Māori than Dad.

'That father of yours thinks he's a Pākehā,' she would growl.

There were times I would help Mary with her phone because it had been cut off. Other times, when she was having trouble with her car I'd be out there in the dead of night, rain, hail or storm, either pushing it to get it started or to get it out of the mud. Other times I was simply helping to straighten her up because she'd had too much to drink at the pub. However, when I turned

17 that all stopped. That's when I was kicked out of home and sent to live with my cousin in Orewa.

There were a lot of changes at home after I was gone. Mum started a new relationship, had a baby and moved down south to manage a bank. She had managed to get Shaun a job for the same bank in a small rural town near Napier. Dad moved in with a woman in Kaukapakapa. Which meant that, at the age of fourteen, my little sister, Katie, had been left at home on her own. Near the end of 1990 I was 18 and allowed back home so that Katie, who was now 15, wouldn't be alone.

Alex's children usually stayed with their grandmother so Katie and I got to know them well. Their nicknames were Pigeon and Papa Bull, and they spent days at our house under Katie's care.

It was an exciting day when Pigeon turned five and started school. From then on, each morning during the week she would walk down to the end of Barr Road with Mary, Papa Bull and Katie. It was from there that she and Katie would catch the school bus.

One morning early in 1991, I joined Katie, Mary and the two little ones at the end of the road. I was meeting up with a friend in Helensville, further south, and together we were heading into town. The school bus driver would often give residents a lift into Helensville, where we could then get another bus into the heart of Auckland.

Alex pulled up in his car to a hero's welcome from his children. It was unusual for him to turn up at this time—he usually visited on the weekends—and we were all happy to see him.

Katie noticed the school bus appear down in the valley and start its climb up the large, steep hill we were standing on. Knowing it would take a couple of minutes for the bus to reach us, Katie crossed the road to the spot where the bus would stop for us to get on. I stayed back, waiting for Pigeon to say goodbye to her family.

Alex leaned out the window of his car and kissed his daughter. Pigeon then kissed her grandmother and said bye to her little brother.

A large twin-trailer truck was loud as it came around the bend at the top of the hill, heading north. I stood back from the side of the road, watching the truck approach.

'Hold Timmy's hand, baby!' Mary called out.

I stretched out my hand for Pigeon to hold onto as I checked behind the passing truck to see if anything was following it. When I looked back Pigeon had run straight past my hand and was now out on the road. The truck smacked into her and roared on.

There was moment of stillness with everyone trying to make sense of what just happened. Then Mary screamed.

Katie collapsed in a heap on the ground. I chased after the truck, trying to find Pigeon—trying to find anything that resembled the beautiful little girl. Hearing Mary's screams, the truck driver braked and pulled over further down the road. He hadn't seen or felt a thing. I ran about looking for Pigeon, then turned away from what I found. Pigeon was no longer there.

Mary ran past me and straight into pounding her fists against the bewildered truck driver, as he climbed down out of the truck.

Alex got out of his car and walked down the road.

I was running around frantically, trying to find a way to change what had just happened.

'Tim, Tim,' Alex said, getting my attention. 'Go and phone an ambulance, boy.'

I ran up Barr Road, up our drive and burst through the door, startling Dad, who had turned up earlier that morning.

'What the bloody hell's going on?' he growled.

I told him what had happened as I phoned 111.

Dad headed down to the scene.

By the time I got back to the end of Barr Road there were cars stopped and more people. Mary was wailing, clutching what was left of Pigeon's lifeless body. Katie was being held by an older girl from school. Someone was moving the school bus on. I looked around and didn't know what to do.

People were looking at me as though I had just turned up and hadn't been there, hadn't seen what happened, like I was a stranger to the moment. All I could think about was that Pigeon was supposed to hold my hand. I wanted to run, get away. I looked at Katie. I wanted to look after my sister, but she was buried in the older girl's embrace.

I got on the school bus and I left. I stayed away all day. I tried to pretend it hadn't happened. I didn't want it to be true, but the image of Pigeon running out onto the road and being hit by the truck kept playing over and over in my head. Every time I closed my eyes it was there. I kept thinking of how it could have been different. How I could have saved Pigeon if only I'd been watching her. How I should have grabbed her.

And I kept thinking of Mary, Alex, Papa Bull and Katie. I knew I would eventually have to face them. There was no avoiding it. That evening I hitched a ride to Kakanui Marae.

When I arrived people were setting up for Pigeon's tangi. They watched me as I entered. Did they know? Did they know I was there that morning? That Pigeon was supposed to hold my hand and that she was little more than an arm's length's from me when she got hit? That I could have saved her?

I chose to stay at the marae rather than go home. I couldn't go near the end of Barr Road for some time following the incident. Mary was warm towards me so it seemed to be okay for me to be there. But I was wary around Alex.

Late one evening he came into the wharenui and lay down next to me. He had been drinking.

'You wanna come and kill a cow with us, Tim?' he asked.

'Eh?' I said. I wasn't sure if I had heard him correctly.

'You wanna come and kill a cow with us?' he repeated.

I was confused. 'Whose cow?' I asked.

'Some farmer's up the road,' he said. 'Don't worry, he won't know. It's dark. We'll just go into the paddock, shoot the cow and get it back here.'

Running around in the middle of the night on some farmer's land with a gun, to shoot and steal a cow, didn't seem to be such a wise thing to do to me. Every farmer in the area had guns. The owner was likely to come out shooting.

'We need the meat to feed everyone.' Alex, nodded at the people crowding the whare.

'Uh nah, I'll just stay here with your mum,' I said.

Part of me wanted to go with Alex. Just to be with him, to support him. I appreciated the fact that he had asked me. However, as the months passed following the tangi I kept my distance from him.

Then one day I was hitchhiking and Alex and his mates pulled up in front of me.

I didn't want to get into the car. I didn't want to face him, but I couldn't reject his offer of a ride. Reluctantly I climbed in.

He pulled the car back onto the road without asking me where I was heading.

'Uh, I'm just going home,' I said.

'No, you're not,' Alex replied. 'You're coming with us.'

He drove me past Barr Road and up to Atuanui, Mount Auckland, to a house where he was staying.

I followed Alex and his friends inside. We sat around a table and had lunch together of fresh sandwiches and hot tea. Alex was good with me. While I was blaming myself for Pigeon's death, Alex wasn't blaming me at all.

Katie also blamed herself for Pigeon's death.

She had wanted Mum to come home after the accident, to be there for her, but Mum refused. Katie and I were left to deal with it on our own. Dad was angry that the accident impacted us so much. Even before the tangi had finished he wanted Katie and me to be over it.

Thoughts of suicide had been a constant companion throughout my teen years, and leading up to that fateful day I'd been pleading to God to end my life. I prayed every night, begging God to take me in my sleep. I wrote about ending my life. I drew about it. I was obsessed. I practised cutting myself, making myself bleed. I loathed and hated everything about me. I believed

I was unlovable and that the world would be better off without me in it. I was so riddled with guilt—guilt over existing and having caused my mother so much grief.

However my desire to end my life changed the day Pigeon died.

Five-year-old little Pigeon had her life taken away. As bad as my existence was and as powerless as I felt, at least I had a chance at a future. Pigeon had been full of life, excited about each day and always playing. How could I even consider suicide when I had a chance for better? I vowed to live for Pigeon, and for all of my friends who had gone. I owed it to them to have a good life and to make the most of my time here in this world.

Whenever thoughts of suicide resurfaced the memory of Pigeon and the vow I'd made to her came with them. As bad as my life had been, I had learned that everything changes. No one knows what tomorrow brings. Every new day—every new sunrise—is a new beginning, a new hope. It is full of possibility and a chance to do things differently.

I chose to live.

RUNNING AWAY

One morning Mum phoned me from work. I was 14, and instead of going to school I had been instructed to stay home and mend the fences around the property to stop Mum's goats from getting out. Mum was furious on the phone because she'd discovered that I had told an older Pākehā cousin that Mum was planning a trip to Nepal India.

It was now trendy to go to exotic places, and Mum's friends were heading off for their Indian adventures, and Mum wanted hers, especially after watching the films, '*A Passage to India*' and '*Heat and Dust*'.

I had just been so excited because there was a chance I might be going on the trip as well, so I'd told my cousin and made her promise to keep it a secret, and especially not to tell Mum. However that promise had obviously been broken.

'How dare you!' Mum snapped. 'I wanted to be the one to tell people!'

'I'm sorry, Mum.'

'Why were you even born?' she growled. 'You ruined my bloody life! I wish I'd never had you! You disgust me! You make me sick!'

In every movie, television programme and story I'd heard as a child your mother was supposed to be the one person in life who had your back, but my mother was no Mother's Day mum.

I tried to plead forgiveness, yet Mum wasn't having it. She continued with a barrage of insults and swear words.

'You wait till I get home!' she snarled, and hung up.

Waiting for her to get home was also waiting for Dad and my siblings to get home, and once they found out I'd hurt Mum they would all be out for me.

I quietly walked upstairs to my room and sat on my bed, contemplating my options. I then rummaged through the cupboards throughout the house, gathering all the bottles and packages of medicines I could find and put them on the dining table with a glass of water. I looked each medicine over. I had no idea what any of them were for, but I figured some of them were probably contraception pills. I doubted they would kill me.

I put the drugs away and went and got a knife. I would often dance around my room to music holding a pair of knives, one over each wrist, and imagine cutting. Now in the moment, though, it was hard to comprehend cutting myself. I had made myself bleed before, but not to that extent. I thought that would be a slow, messy and painful way to go.

So I put the knife away and went into the garage and got some rope. I took the rope upstairs and strung it up over the rafters in my room. I grabbed a chair from the dining table and placed underneath. I stood on the chair and put my head through the noose. I'd had friends from school who'd done this. I trembled. I felt so alone.

I believed that taking my own life would make Mum happy. She would wear the sympathy like a badge of honour, and I wouldn't be around any longer to burden her. Mum had always been at me, telling me how bad I was, that she wished I wasn't there, that I was nothing but trouble.

I didn't want to die though. I just wanted to be loved.

I took my head out from the noose, collapsed on my bed and sobbed. 'God, God,' I cried. 'Why won't you help me?'

It was desperation that had been keeping me alive up to this point. I was desperate for a mother's love and to be wanted.

The day was quiet. I lay back on the bed and watched the clouds out the window. Mum would be home later and I would have to face her loathing and disgust, and her fists.

I looked at the noose hanging from the rafters. I wasn't going to let Mum win. I wasn't going to die for her. I was going to live.

I got up, put away the rope and chair, and then got out my schoolbag. I was running away.

I packed some clothes, a knife, a pair of nunchaku and the most valuable thing I had—my collection of GI Joe comics and ninja magazines. I had bought them from second-hand bookstores on the days when I'd wagged school and gone into town with mates. I had gotten the money from shoplifting and selling the goods to second-hand shops.

Before leaving I said goodbye to Sid the Doberman, the cats and the horses. I walked down State Highway 16, making sure to hide whenever I heard a car. My plan was to get to Kaukapakapa and catch the bus from there into Auckland City. I was heading for my Nana Tipene. I would stay with her. Or maybe Aunty Joy. I wasn't sure yet. The most important thing was just to get away. My family weren't going to hurt me anymore.

As the afternoon drew on I was aware that the school buses would soon be coming my way. There were also certain houses I had to avoid. One in particular belonged to the principal of one of the local primary schools. He drank at the pub with Mum. There was even a rumour circulating through the community that they had slept together. If he saw me I was certain he'd tell Mum.

I decided to cut inland and walk over the farms. This made the trip a lot longer. I got thirsty and had no drinking water, so I drank from troughs with the cows. This wasn't a good idea because I ended up with a tummy bug in the days following.

When evening arrived I made my way back to the highway and continued along it. At the top of a hill I went up a bank and found a sheltered spot beneath the trees that overlooked the road. It was out of the wind and dry. I nestled down for the night. As I lay there, looking up at the branches and the night sky, I thought about where I was heading. I thought about Nana. At that time, other than Uncle Blake, we had nothing to do with the whānau. Now and then we would run into some of them when we were out and about, but I hadn't seen Nana for years.

Now, beneath the trees, I was wondering what Nana and Aunty Joy would do if I just suddenly turned up on their doorsteps? Would they still consider me, a white boy, whānau? Would Nana even remember me?

There were other relatives, like Uncle Blake, that I could go to. But Uncle would just send me straight back, and probably with a kick up the arse for upsetting Mum.

The police sure weren't going to help. The local cops were well aware of what was happening in my home and they hadn't done anything about it. They drank at the pub with Dad. There was no family violence or child abuse intervention in my day.

As for my school, they were only ever interested in punishing me.

I had mates who knew about my home. I was sure they would help me. They would probably give me money for a bus trip and their families might even put me up for a night, but there was little else they could do.

Besides living on the street I had nowhere to go, and as much as I wanted to get away I also wanted to go back. The more Mum rejected me the more I craved her love and approval.

I curled up and tried to get warm. Eventually I fell asleep. When I woke in the morning I had come to the conclusion that my only option was to go home.

I waited until the flow of people going to work and school had died down, then started for home. I wasn't hiding from cars anymore, and thirty minutes into my walk a car pulled up in front of me. It was a local mum.

I took a deep breath. I knew what was about to happen. Mum would have milked the situation for all she could get so most of the community would know what I had done. I had messed up and Mum was now in the position to show everyone that I was the problem teenager in our home and that this is what she had to put up with, and of course the community would have rallied behind her.

The local mum told me to get into her car. I sat in the front passenger seat, closing the door behind me. As soon as she had pulled back onto the highway the woman went into a verbal onslaught of how disgraceful my behaviour was. She ranted on about how ungrateful and selfish I was, what a problem and disappointment I was for my mother and how I had let her down.

'You should be ashamed of yourself,' the woman said. 'You don't know how lucky you are.'

I never said a word. I knew there was no point—this woman wasn't going to listen to me.

I thanked her when she dropped me off at the end of my road. I knew she would soon be on the phone, informing the neighbourhood about how I had turned up broken and regretful.

I got home to find no one was there. When the family did turn up nothing was said. They simply carried on as though it had never happened.

¤ ¤ ¤

One morning not long after this, Katie had told me that I needed to get ready to go out. She said that Dad was taking us over to south Auckland to see Aunty Joy. I didn't believe it. It was only Dad, Shaun, Katie and I that got in the car. Mum didn't come. I was quiet all the way to Otara and even when we pulled up at Aunty Joy's house I was thinking that Dad will probably turn the car around and take us back home. I was too scared to get my hopes up.

Before Dad opened his door he warned us that Aunty was sick with cancer and that she wasn't expected to live for much longer. When we got inside I wasn't sure how to be. Uncle Andy led us to Aunties room. Dad was right about her being sick. She wasn't the strong woman that I remembered. She remembered me, but there was an awkwardness in the room. There was a lot unsaid between the adults.

When we left I didn't want to go. I was certain that this would be the last time that I would see Aunty Joy alive. I was right.

When Aunty Joy passed away I went and stayed with Uncle Blake. I was thinking that by doing so I might get to go to the tangihanga, but it turned out that Uncle Blake had issues with Aunty too. We worked instead. I spent the whole day of her funeral mourning and not being able to show it.

¤ ¤ ¤

Mum did go to India and Nepal, and I got to go with her, but it wasn't the mother and son trip that I had hoped for. I spent the majority of the time on my own with the locals.

'I didn't come here to hang out with you!' Mum told me.

She would send me off to go exploring by myself and I wasn't to come back till late so that she could do what she wanted.

This was exactly why I was the one Mum had chosen for the trip. I was her cover story when it came to the family. As far as they were concerned Mum and I had come to India to see our Uncle Norman, the missionary.

One night Mum and I were woken by a knock on the door of our room. It was when we were staying in a guest house in Kathmandu. Mum got up and answered the door. It was a man and I could hear him trying to get Mum to go with him. Some other things were said that I couldn't hear, then the door was closed and Mum got back into her bed.

'It's alright,' she said. 'He had the wrong room. Go back to sleep.'

I turned over and closed my eyes.

A short time later I woke to the door closing. I looked about to see that I was alone. Mum had gone. She didn't return till much later in the morning.

This was why Shaun and Katie weren't the ones to accompany Mum to Nepal and India. Mum couldn't have had her, '*Heat and Dust*', experience with my siblings there. They were too close to Mum and they wouldn't have let her out of their sight. None of the family listened to me, so Mum was free to experience India.

I had a wonderful time with the locals. While we were in India Mum decided to extend our trip. However she failed to inform Dad on time, so the poor bugger was left waiting at the airport. Oh the drama.

Shaun and Katie didn't miss out. They got to go to Hawaii and other exciting places without me.

KENJI

Mum decided to get a little Māori boy. She said it was for Dad because he had always wanted a son. I had thought Shaun and I were Dad's sons, but apparently we weren't the right colour. Mum was keen on fostering. She raved about it being another source of income, and she wanted to add to her collection of rescued, less fortunate beings.

Social Welfare deemed us a good family for a child. Before the social worker came around to interview us Mum had given us kids instructions on how to behave. It was the usual don't speak unless you are spoken to and only give answers that make us look good as a family. Mum was big on keeping up appearances. She tended to get what she wanted and there were harsh penalties for anyone who let her down.

Kenji was of Māori and Japanese descent. He was a tiny 10-year-old who had already had a hard life before coming to live with us. I was fifteen at the time. The story that Mum told everyone was that Kenji's mother had worked the streets in the city and had met Kenji's father when his ship was docked at the wharves. Kenji had been in the welfare system all his life, had lived in numerous homes and had been abused.

Kenji moved into my bedroom. I had always shared my room with my dog Herbie, who was still alive at this point, and Sid the Doberman. But the bed they had used now became Kenji's and the dogs went into the garage. I wasn't happy about that because it had been a comfort to have Herbie and Sid in my room. I was also aware that I had now dropped further down the pecking order. Instead of being at the bottom in a family of five, I was now last in a family of six.

Mum wanted Kenji and me to get on with one another. However she had little patience, so rather than waiting for a connection to naturally develop between the two of us Mum resorted to forcing Kenji and me to play together. She would tell us to wrestle one another on the bed as she stood over us watching. She would even use a timer and Kenji and I weren't to stop wrestling until the time had run out. Now and then she would leave the room, but shortly return to make sure we were still going. It was weird and uncomfortable, particularly since both Kenji and I had been victims of sexual abuse.

Regardless of Mum's efforts, over time Kenji and I became brothers. I now had my own student to teach martial arts to and Kenji loved it.

Kenji was Mum's showpiece for a while. Everywhere we went Mum would put him front and centre. She would recount how she had singlehandedly saved the poor wretched creature and how better off he was for being under her care. Kenji was her project and Mum was desperate to feel good about herself. It didn't last long though, and just like with all her previous projects Mum lost interest and moved on to other things. She couldn't risk getting close to anyone or anything as it rattled the ghosts of her past.

Kenji liked the attention he got from our rich Pākehā cousins. I knew that wouldn't last either. Kenji didn't realise, but he had just taken my position as a source of entertainment. Sure enough, it wasn't long before it was just him and me wandering the streets of Leigh together.

Kenji was a tough boy. He had only been with us a couple of weeks when he decided to try it on with Dad. Dad was giving Kenji a telling off, but Kenji ignored Dad and went to walk past him.

Katie and I looked at one another.

I cringed. *No, no Kenji*, I thought. *Don't do that.*

It was too late. Dad grabbed Kenji by the top of his shirt. While holding the shirt he punched Kenji in the chest with the same hand, forcing the little boy back. Dad then wrenched Kenji forward and stopped his fist so that Kenji's face collided with it.

It was a technique Dad had mastered on me.

'Don't you fuck with me, boy!' Dad growled at Kenji.

The fear on Kenji's face as he looked up at Dad told Katie and me that the boy finally understood he'd been placed in a house of horror.

Dad never liked Kenji. Kenji was Māori, and Dad didn't like the Māori boy within himself. Dad resented the Māori world. It had hurt and betrayed him. As far as he was concerned Kenji was just another punching bag to project his self loathing onto. He made the poor kid's life a living hell.

¤ ¤ ¤

Once I turned seventeen Mum kicked me out. Now and then I was allowed back home to visit, but only when Mum was wanting something from me.

One such occasion was when she and Dad were wanting me to retrieve Kenji from Kakanui Marae. Twelve-year-old Kenji had gone there to get away from the violence and abuse at home. Now that I was no longer around he had become the primary target for Mum and Dad's aggression.

The hau kāinga (local people of the marae) had made it clear that none of the family were permitted onto the marae to get Kenji, other than me. Mum and Dad weren't wanting to go near the place anyway.

In the wharenui I was told off by the elders for the violence and abuse at home. They wanted me to give my assurance that Kenji would be looked after and kept safe in my family's care. These people knew my family. They knew I was in no position to give assurances like that. I was a teenager who'd been kicked out of home. I couldn't even keep myself safe around my family.

Knowing that I couldn't go back home without Kenji, I told the hau kāinga what they wanted to hear. When Kenji and I turned up later that evening Mum and Dad said nothing. I got to stay for a couple of days, but then I had to leave Kenji to his fate. It was the last time I would see him.

A week later Kenji grabbed his opportunity to get away in the middle of Auckland City. Dad had gone into town and taken Katie and Kenji with him. When Dad pulled up at a red light Kenji jumped out the back door and bolted.

For a while he would phone home every now and then, hoping to catch me or Katie. But Dad answered the phone one day and told Kenji to fuck off and to never phone again.

¤ ¤ ¤

On Christmas Day in 2014 I received an amazing gift—a text from a man looking for his long-lost brother. It was Kenji. We spoke on the phone that morning and the next day he came over to my house. Kenji and I hadn't seen each other for almost thirty years. There were a lot of hugs.

Kenji had searched for me online. and found an author who ran a programme called Warrior Kids, but he hadn't been sure if it was me.

'I tried to make a big enough noise so you could find me,' I said.

Kenji was amazed with what I had done with my life. He said he was proud of me, and explained that we had gone in completely opposite directions. While I had gone for healing, changing the past and making a difference, Kenji had ended up in a gang, had spent time behind bars and had battled drug addiction.

I wasn't into judgements. I could have so easily have ended up going the same road as Kenji, and I nearly did. Looking at him reminded me of how far I had come and how much I had faced. He also reminded me of all the incarcerated adults who were abused as children, and how that abuse had never been addressed either by the adults who had done it or by society.

When we spoke about the past it became apparent to me that Kenji blamed himself for the abuse and trauma he'd received as a child. Like me, he believed he was a rotten kid who deserved every bad thing that had ever happened to him. It is common for children who grow up in abusive homes to believe that the abuse is all their fault. It comes down to the perception of power and the need for hope for change. If something is wrong with me I can change it, but if something is wrong with the adults around me I am powerless to do anything about it. If there are behaviours of mine that are causing my parent to not love me then if I can fix those behaviours I'll be loved, but if the love from the parent simply isn't there, regardless of my behaviour, then there is no fixing it.

I told Kenji he hadn't been a bad kid. 'I'm your older brother,' I said. 'I was there for part of your life. You were abused and mistreated in our home, and before you came to live with us you'd already had a long history of being hurt and abused. None of that was ever your fault, Kenji. It was those messed up adults.'

Kenji wasn't ready to hear that. His whole life had been built on the belief that he was bad.

'I'm sorry, Kenji,' I said, acknowledging this and apologising for any part I had played in the abuse.

He didn't want to talk about it anymore. However I kept saying sorry until he heard me.

'You were the one who looked after me, Tim,' he said. 'That's what I remember about you. You were there for me.'

'I wish I could have looked after you more,' I replied.

'It's all good, bro, it's all good,' he said.

Kenji and I looked for any reason to get together that year. We celebrated one another's birthdays and went to different places. Kenji even attended my weekly teen and adult class, training with me and his nephew and niece. My son and daughter adored their new-found uncle and his partner.

In 2015 we lost Uncle Tom, one of Nana Tipene's four special needs sons. Kenji came with the kids and me to the tangihanga at Naumai Marae. On the way up north we had to stop a couple of times so Kenji could have a smoke as he was so nervous. I had to keep giving my brother pep talks because he was worried about seeing the rest of the family. There was a lot of whānau who had never even met him.

On the day of the funeral Dad, Shaun and Katie turned up. They were surprised to see Kenji.

'So this is where I got all my craziness from, eh?' Kenji smiled at Dad, and he gave him a hug.

I could see Dad was uncomfortable. It was hard enough for him having to face the whānau, let alone another son he'd abused.

Shaun was perplexed as to why Kenji was there.

'Your time with us wasn't good,' Shaun said to him. 'You were treated so badly and hurt by this family.'

'Yeah, I know,' Kenji replied.

'Why would you want anything to do with us?' Shaun asked.

'That's the past,' Kenji answered. 'It's all good.'

HIGH SCHOOL

I had grown up wearing glasses, but after two eye operations I only had to wear glasses for reading and writing. So when the family moved from Herald Island to Makarau I started at Kaukapakapa School with a new confidence, and for once in my life I was popular rather than infamous. I enjoyed the attention, but it didn't last long. When I started high school the following year my face was full of acne.

Many kids, especially the girls pointed out the change.

'Wow, you used to be handsome,' they said. 'You're not handsome anymore.'

Boys were also amused.

'Hey, Tim!' they'd cry, 'Here's a map of the Himalayas to help you shave! How else are you going to get around those mountains on your face?'

My acne was so bad that one year a teacher phoned Mum and requested that she take me to the doctor about it. Mum wasn't impressed.

I had always been led to believe that my failure at school was my fault. It was what my school reports said, and my teachers, and my family. Therefore I believed that if I applied myself and put more effort into my work I would do better. I told myself that it didn't matter that Shaun had started high school with a stylish haircut, cool Nomad shoes and the best gear, while I was starting with a crewcut, the cheapest Velcro shoes and lesser gear. Thinking the power was all in my hands, I began high school with a mind to improve my schooling.

During my first week I arrived home one afternoon and headed straight upstairs.

Dad was on a night shift that day so was also home. 'Where you going?' he yelled.

'I'm going to do my homework,' I replied.

'No, you're not,' he said. 'Get out there and mow those lawns.'

I never questioned Dad or Mum because they always saw it as answering back, and I got hit for answering back. But on this occasion I was thinking that Dad might have overlooked the fact that I had started high school. When Shaun started high school he had been relieved of jobs such as mowing the lawns so he could focus more on his schoolwork.

'I've got homework to do, Dad,' I said, coming back down the stairs.

'What!' Dad growled, flexing his arms as he gave me his full attention.

I was on the edge and had to tread carefully. 'My science teacher said my homework has to be in tomorrow,' I tried to explain.

'You tell your teacher that I said you're not doing any homework!' Dad instructed. 'And if he has a problem with that, you tell him to phone me! Now get out there and mow those bloody lawns!'

A couple of days later the science teacher went through the roll, calling out names of students who had failed to turn in their homework.

'Timothy Tippanee, where is your homework?' he asked.

'My dad told me not to do it,' I replied.

'Detention,' the teacher said.

I couldn't win. If I did my homework and went against my parents I'd get punched in the head. If I didn't do my homework I was going to get into trouble at school, and when I brought a bad report home that was another hit in the head.

And now I'd had my first detention. Still, I was determined I would never get another one.

That was just wishful thinking. My lunchtimes were often spent sitting in a classroom copying pages from history books. To tell the truth I actually enjoyed detention. The room was quiet and I found the history books interesting. It was one of the only times I got to read. Detention also meant that I was able to avoid interacting socially with the other teens—something I was finding difficult to do.

¤ ¤ ¤

One day at school boys in my year were skiting about having burnt their initials on concrete with petrol. Apparently anyone who was cool had done it.

I hadn't done it. So I went home, got the petrol can, poured out my initials on the driveway and lit it with a match. I stood back and watched, but I couldn't see anything burning. Disappointed, I decided to try burning my initials in some short grass. Again nothing much happened. The boys at school had made out that it was amazing, but it wasn't working for me.

I eyed the long brown grass in the paddock next door.

That would work, I thought.

I jumped the fence, poured out my name and lit it. I couldn't see a thing. Obviously the boys had been having me on. I returned to the house, put the petrol can back in the garage and went inside.

A couple of minutes later Shaun burst out of the toilet. 'Timmy, what the hell have you done!'

'What!' I frowned.

'The paddock's on fire!' he yelled, bounding out the house.

He grabbed a shovel. I grabbed the spade. We jumped the fence and started pounding the burning grass. Katie kept bringing us buckets of water. It took us a while but we managed to put the fire out. The paddock now had a large bare, black patch.

'Man, Timmy!' Shaun growled.

'Far out,' Katie added. 'You're a dick.'

Thankfully neither of them told Mum or Dad. They knew what would have happened to me if they had. There were many instances over the years where my siblings protected me. From that point on, though, Shaun and Katie believed I had a problem with fire, that I was a pyromaniac. Yet they weren't even home the day I decided to make Molotov cocktails. I had fireballs exploding all over the driveway.

When I was in my early twenties and back home looking after Katie and her toddler, I decided to spend the night in the bush on the family property. In amongst the trees I lit a little fire and snuggled up beneath a couple of blankets under the stars. It was wonderful and I had a good sleep. In the morning I dug over the fire, making sure it was out. I then went back home, got myself organised and hitchhiked to my girlfriend's place.

Later that day she drove me home. When we pulled into Barr Road we found a string of cars lining the side.

'Why are they all here?' my girlfriend queried.

I had no idea.

When we drove by the cars I could see local people I knew in each of them. I was smiling and waving to them all; however none of them were smiling and waving back. Their faces were sour. Obviously something had happened.

Blossom, the mother of my mates Rueben and Bobby, pointed back at the bush on our land. I turned to see four fire engines and a water truck parked in our paddock. The bush was on fire.

'Shit,' I said, looking at my girlfriend.

I knew I was in a whole lot of trouble.

This was the day I learnt about peat and how fire can burn undetected, underground. Everyone was pissed off with me. The firemen working in the hot summer sun, the locals who were fearful for their homes that were in the bush further down the hill—and Dad, who clearly wanted to use the shovel he was holding on my ass, but couldn't because of all the witnesses.

I spent twenty-four hours on fire watch with Dad and a local fireman. We were constantly dampening hotspots. Any sign of smoke or smouldering and we pounced on it with shovels. Even after twenty-four hours we still had to keep an eye on it. Because of my youth and ignorance, and the fact that Dad drank at the pub with a number of the firemen, there was no bill. But I wasn't to be lighting fires around there again.

'You and fire, eh, Timmy,' Katie taunted.

I hadn't meant to start a bushfire.

When it had all calmed down and was back to just Katie, her boy and me at home, I turned to my little nephew.

'Now you just remember, nephew,' I said. 'Your uncle got you four fire engines and a water truck.'

Katie laughed. 'Bloody hell, Timmy,' she said. 'You're a dick.'

THE MAGIC ROOM

When Shaun began fifth form (year 11), Mum and Dad went out of their way to prepare him for a serious year of education. They were determined that nothing was going to get in the way of him reaching his full potential. Uncle Blake even presented Shaun with a new schoolbag and all the latest school equipment for him to succeed. It was Shaun's initiation into higher learning. So when it came to my year 11 I couldn't wait to receive my new school bag and gear to conquer school certificate. However I didn't get anything.

Instead when I got ready to go to school on the first week Dad frowned at me. 'Where are you going?'

'To school,' I said.

'No, you're not,' Dad replied. 'You're staying home to paint your mother's fence.'

A week later, after two coats of white paint on Mum's picket fence, Dad turned up with buckets of brown paint for the house.

I was baffled. I had thought that 5th form was supposed to be an important year.

I was absent for so long that in the end the college phoned. I was the only one home at the time. I had stopped painting and come inside to have some lunch when the phone went.

The office lady asked to speak to Mr or Mrs Tippanee.

I told her that neither of my parents were home.

'We would like to know if Timothy Tippanee is still attending college?' the woman asked.

I looked around. 'I don't know,' I said. 'I'll have to ask my parents.'

When Dad got home from work I told him about the phone call, and about the school wanting to know if I was still attending.

'You better go to school tomorrow,' he said.

Even though I was on my own when it came to my education I was determined not to fail year 11. I returned to school with enthusiasm. I didn't need a new bag and all the gear. I was certain that all I needed was the belief that I could succeed. Even with maths, my most feared subject, I was sure that if I applied myself I would get there.

I was thrilled to discover that I had been placed in Mr Grayson's class. Mr Grayson was regarded as a rock star of maths. He was popular among the students, with many of them on first-name basis with him. They would cry out his name whenever he was strutting through the school. Mr Grayson never just walked—he strutted, with his head held high and a scarf often flung about his neck. He wore long hair and had an attitude to match. Shaun was one of the many students who looked up to Mr Grayson, saying he was a brilliant teacher, and brilliant at maths.

I was grateful to be in Mr Grayson's class. If anyone could help me with maths it had to be him, and since my brother had a great relationship with him, surely this would flow onto me?

It had been a few weeks since school had started and the class was well established when I walked in for the first time. I found a seat at the back of the room where I wouldn't be too visible. I hated being put on the spot with a maths question. Teachers had often made me stand up in front of the other students to answer equations. I never knew the answers so I just guessed. This made the students laugh, and the teacher would always ridicule or belittle me in some way.

The famous Mr Grayson entered the room to a hero's welcome from the students. He took his place at the front of the class. After some chitchat with his fan club of adoring pupils he got into writing on the board.

Right, this is it, I thought. *Time for some serious learning.*

Finally I was going to understand maths.

I studied the maths equations Mr Grayson was writing up. I couldn't make sense of any of them. I didn't even have any idea if the equations were going up, down or to the side. There were also letters in it. I hated seeing letters in maths. Did that mean that numbers were going to be a part of writing? I was confident with letters, but I wasn't confident with numbers.

I looked at the other students. Were they getting this?

'There it is,' Mr Grayson said, turning to the class.

He referenced a page number in the thick maths textbook which everyone immediately started turning to. Some students put up their hand for assistance.

Relieved that I wasn't the only one who didn't understand, I put my hand up too. Maybe I wasn't behind everybody else as much as I'd thought.

Mr Grayson glanced around the room at the hands in the air. His eyes came to me. An expression of shock and bewilderment filled his face. He walked over to his desk and checked the roll, obviously verifying that I was where I was supposed to be. Taking another glance at me, Mr Grayson went to a nearby student and assisted her.

I waited. When Mr Grayson had finished he straightened up. 'Right, who else requires help?'

I raised my hand in unison with other students.

Mr Grayson went to the nearest one.

This went on for a while until I was the last one left with my hand up.

I watched Mr Grayson take a deep breath before he walked to the back of the room and stood over me.

'Yes?' he asked, peering down.

I looked at the textbook on my desk and then up at Mr Grayson.

'What part don't you understand?' Mr Grayson inquired.

I looked at the textbook again. 'All of it,' I said.

Mr Grayson huffed. He leaned over me and started to try and explain the equation. I watched his mouth move as he talked, but it was as though he was speaking another language. I didn't understand anything he was saying.

Obviously realising this, Mr Grayson pulled back. 'I don't know how you got into my class,' he said, shaking his head.

The other students turned around to watch.

Mr Grayson looked at me firmly. 'When you are in my class you sit at the back,' he directed. 'Do whatever you like—I don't care. Just don't interrupt my class and don't put your hand up.'

And with that Mr Grayson walked away.

I could feel my face burning red with the other students looking on. I watched the teacher return to the front of the class and thought, *I guess I'm not going to be good at maths then.*

My hopes of finally getting to understand maths fell away. I had also just been rejected by the most popular teacher in the school. What did that say about me?

I turned to the back of my maths book and instead of thinking numbers I started thinking words. Words were something I did understand, and through words I left Mr Grayson and his classroom behind as I delved into another world—the world of story writing.

The next time I entered Mr Grayson's math's class he stood tall.

'You're not in here anymore,' he said, triumphantly.

The students all looked at me.

'Go to the office,' Mr Grayson said. 'They'll tell you where you're supposed to be.'

The office sent me to a small room where there were only a handful of students and a female teacher. I had been in many special classes just like this one ever since I started school at five.

'There was a mix-up,' the teacher said. 'This class is more your level.'

With this chance to understand mathematics, I started to feel hopeful again.

I took my place at a table and looked over the worksheet of New Zealand Maths in front of me. It was supposed to be a simpler form of maths. While I understood some of it, most of it I didn't. The problem I had was that whenever I looked at numbers my brain would just tune out. The teacher sat and worked with me.

I attended this little class for a couple of weeks and over that time I noticed that the number of students began to dwindle. Students who caught up in their learning were able to re-join their fellow students in the normal maths curriculum classes. Eventually I was the only student left in the special maths class. It was just me and the teacher.

And then it was just me. I arrived at the room one day to find a worksheet sitting on the desk with a note from the teacher telling me to complete it.

'Just do the best you can,' the note said.

I studied the sheet. A couple of the equations I understood, but as for the rest of them I had no idea. I decided to turn to God. With each equation I would look up and ask God for the answer. The first numbers that popped into my head I took as divine inspiration and I wrote them down.

When I came back to the class the next day my worksheet had been marked and left on the table. It had red crosses all over it. I had gotten every answer wrong, even the ones I had thought I understood. A new maths worksheet had been left for me to complete, along with a new note.

'Try harder,' it said.

So I prayed harder to God for the answers.

When I returned the next time I realised God obviously had more important things to do because he certainly wasn't helping me with my maths. I had gotten every answer wrong again.

There was a new maths worksheet and another note telling me I wasn't trying hard enough.

This went on for a couple of weeks until one day I turned up and found my maths worksheet unmarked and no new note or worksheet. I figured the teacher must be absent, so I took my science book out of my bag, turned to the back and wrote a story.

The next time I attended maths the same worksheet was still sitting there, unmarked. It was the same the next time. In fact, I never saw the teacher again, my worksheet was never marked, and there were never any new worksheets. I presumed that this little room was where the school wanted me to be. Either that or they had simply forgotten about me.

I decided to make good of a bad situation. My maths time became my writing time. It was where I could write whatever I wanted to. Rather than being something I dreaded, maths class was now a place where I wanted to be. It was a time just for me. I wrote and I wrote, cramming as much writing as I could into the hour I had. I would be writing so fast my hand would get sore and I would have to shake it and massage it to get it working again.

That little room became my magic room. It was exactly where I needed to be. Through my writing I was able to leave the harshness of the world. I could transcend everyday life and dwell in imaginary worlds where I was loved. My writing also allowed me to explore my life—the violence and abuse, the rejection and feelings of being different—and to make sense of it all. In this magic room I was a writer. A craftsman developing his craft.

When I was twelve I had come across a woman up at Leigh sitting behind an easel painting the Leigh Harbour. She sat in silence. I had been impressed with her work and the peacefulness that surrounded her. She was happy to let me watch as she masterfully swished the brush about the canvas.

'Are you an artist?' I asked.

'Yes,' she said.

'I would like to be an artist,' I said. 'How do you become one?'

She smiled at me. 'If you want to become an artist then you have to do it every day,' she said.

Her words have stayed with me. As much as I loved art as a kid, my experiences of art at high school had put me off it. However no one could put me off writing, because my standard 4 teacher, Miss Foote, had told me that I was a writer, and no one was kinder, warmer or more genuine than Miss Foote. So here I was writing every day, writing whenever I had the chance.

In my magic room I wrote poems and love letters for all the girls I liked.

The problem was that while my poems and love letters all started off warm and romantic, they would inevitably lead down a dark path because I was struggling to come to terms with my troubled life. I would go from writing about how beautiful a girl's eyes and hair were, how her voice caressed my heart and she was all that I wanted to know, and then descend into how life sucked and fuck the world and all its people.

I would present my poems and letters to the girls, striving to impress them with my word prowess. And they were impressed—with the first part at least. The girls would smile and their interest would open to me as they read of my crush on them. But as they neared the end of the poem their faces would change, the smile would fade and they would give the poem back.

'I don't think so,' they would say, turning away. 'You've got issues.'

¤ ¤ ¤

Our home at Makarau was remote and miles from anywhere. My world as a teen was small and isolated. Every weekend I was stuck at home. I wasn't allowed to go out to parties or socialise with other kids. While Mum was going to parties herself, she used the strict doctrine of our old church to keep me on the straight and narrow. Basically I had three rules—stay home, work around the property and don't touch the food.

There were periods of my schooling where I didn't have many friends and spent my lunchtimes walking the school alone but one day a friend, Michael, came up to me and told me he needed my help. He and an older boy, Carl, had been talking tough to each other and now they were going to have a fist fight. Michael didn't feel confident facing the year 13 student so he wanted me to do it for him. Not wanting to let my friend down, I said I would take care of it.

I had no idea what the issue was between Michael and Carl, nor did I know how it had started, but I wanted to be a loyal friend. Mum and Dad had made me an enforcer when I was at primary school. They had instructed me to beat up any kid that messed with Katie. Now here I was at high school fulfilling the role again.

Michael set everything up, telling me when and where I was supposed to strike. He knew where Carl was going to be, and on the day Michael and some of his other mates came face to face with Carl on his own in the corridor.

Michael started mouthing off at Carl, who retaliated. I was watching through the windows of the double doors at the end of the corridor.

The two teenage boys started to push one another. This was my cue. I burst through the doors, big and staunch, and thinking I was tough.

As I approached I told the 7th former to leave my friend alone and threatened to smack him over. Carl took off, heading for the opposite end of the corridor. This wasn't part of the plan. I was supposed to face off with the older boy, but he was getting away. I ran after him. Michael and his mates followed.

Carl entered the 7th form common room and stayed there with his girlfriend. I tried to push in to get him, but other 7th formers blocked my path and refused to let me, so I waited outside. The bell rang, signalling the end of lunch, but that wasn't going to stop me. As Michael and his friends went off to class I stayed, determined to see this through.

I stood in the middle of the court and yelled at Carl to come out and face me. I could hear other students in the common room giving Carl a hard time, telling him to go outside and fight me.

'Don't be scared,' they said. 'Shame! Loser! What a wuss.'

I looked around and found I was the only one outside. Everybody else was in their classrooms. I could see students and teachers at class windows, watching me. They had all seen me yelling and carrying on in the middle of the court.

My face started to burn. I didn't feel so tough now. I felt like an idiot.

I turned and walked away, going instead to the magic room, my little maths room. There were no maths sheets to fill in again I pulled out an exercise book from my bag, but I couldn't write. I just sat there thinking about Carl. The voices of the 7th formers ridiculing him and egging him on to fight echoed through my head. Some of the girls had yelled out to me to beat Carl up.

I didn't even know this Carl. I had only just learnt his name. I had nothing against him. Why were people wanting me to hurt this boy? Why were so many against him?

I knew how it felt not to be liked. To be an outsider. I had threatened this boy. What was I thinking? This was not the person I wanted to be. I played the incident over and over in my head, me yelling and carrying on in the middle of the school, trying to be tough and fight some poor kid. I was ashamed of myself. I was better than this.

I wasn't angry at Carl. I was angry at Mum and Dad for abusing, rejecting and hurting me. And I was angry at the school for not caring.

'Lacks confidence. Could be a class leader if he applied himself,' a teacher had written on my report during my first year of high school. I was constantly bullied at school then. My face was covered in acne. When the so-called popular students ridiculed me in class right in front of that teacher she didn't intervene, she didn't stop it. I had put so much effort into that teacher's class and she wrote 'could be a class leader if he applied himself'.

Apparently, I was supposed to be a teenager who had everything going for him. I was supposed to have come from a good home with parents who loved me, and who had instilled in me the confidence to succeed. But that wasn't me. I couldn't magically change my circumstances and be different on my own, and no one else was taking the time to work with me or help me. Especially not my high school teachers.

Yet as I sat there in my little magic room I knew I had done wrong. When the bell rang at the end of class, signalling the end of the day, I went looking for Carl.

Of course, Carl had assumed I would be looking for him and had taken off. However I managed to find Carl's girlfriend. I asked her to tell Carl I was sorry. That I was a complete idiot for what I'd done to him. I told her to tell Carl that I was angry at my dad and not at him.

'Please tell him I'm sorry,' I repeated.

That night I couldn't stop worrying about Carl. I had unintentionally colluded with others in ostracising this boy just as I had been, time and time again. During my first year at high school an older boy I knew had committed suicide because he had been ostracised and I had never forgotten him.

My message to his girlfriend got through though, and from that point on I had a new friend. Whenever Carl saw me he would wave out and call my name. It continued beyond school. As an adult I would be walking down the main drag of Helensville and a car would go by, tooting, and there was Carl behind the wheel, waving and calling out to me.

I was thankful for the offer of friendship and I appreciated that Carl hadn't held ill feelings towards me. Yet I still felt ashamed for having threatened him.

CRAZY NINJA

'You have a reputation for being really bad,' Katie said to me one day. 'But you're not bad at all.'

At school I was seen as someone not to mess with. Kids knew I'd not only gone up ranks in Go Shintai Kai Karate and Judo, I had attended the first ever Togakure-Ryū ninjutsu seminar in New Zealand, beginning my training to be a ninja. There were also stories of my violent home life and of me taking out my rage on the community through smashing and vandalising. I wasn't doing well at school and was known for getting into trouble. I was seen as someone who was unstable and unpredictable. I liked that because it kept people away. However the reputation of me being a bad kid was really a projection put on me by my family, school and community. In reality I was just a traumatised kid who was struggling to cope and in need of love.

One afternoon my mate, Joe, came over to my house. Our house was often the place for other kids to come to because my parents were never home.

Joe and I were in my room mucking about and chatting.

'You know what we should do?' Joe said, changing the course of the conversation.

'What?' I asked.

'We should get a couple of shotguns and go to school and shoot everybody.'

'What?' I smiled, thinking it was a joke.

'I'm serious,' Joe assured me. 'We should go to school with some guns and shoot as many as we can.'

'Why?' I asked.

'You know they don't like you, right?' Joe said. 'You know they all think you're weird?'

'Do they?'

'Yeah, they think you're crazy.'

'Why do they think I'm crazy?' I queried further.

'Because ... you know,' Joe muttered. 'You're different. You don't have many friends. You always keep to yourself and you're not really good at anything. You don't have much going for you.'

I could see him looking at the acne that covered much of my face. 'So why do you want to kill everybody?' I asked.

'Because they're all dickheads,' he snapped. 'They all think they're better than everybody else.'

It was obvious he was talking about the popular kids who appeared to run everything at school. Even the staff supported them, openly celebrating them in front of all the other students who didn't measure up. These students were the sporting champions of the school or the ones whose parents were influential in the community. You had to be a certain type of kid to be deemed worthy of such status, or even to hang out with them.

'You could do most of the shooting,' Joe said.

'Eh?' I frowned.

'Well, you could start it off,' he said. 'Then I'll join in.'

Joe had obviously given it a lot of thought. He went into great detail, telling me he had access to guns, explaining how we could get them into school unnoticed, the exact location in the school where the bloodshed would start, and the path that we would take during the massacre.

'Nah,' I said, 'I'm not doing that.'

Joe looked disappointed.

I had been humiliated, taunted and bullied at school, but as much as I was angry at those kids I wasn't going to shoot them. If anything, that would only prove they were right about me being a loser, a weirdo and strange.

And they weren't right.

¤ ¤ ¤

The day I met Angus I rubbed a mince pie in his hair. As soon as I'd done it I regretted it because although Angus joked about it he went bright red with embarrassment and the other boys laughed at him. This told me that Angus was someone who got picked on, and I hadn't meant to single him out.

I had found the unwrapped, intact pie lying on the ground. Someone had obviously dropped it. I thought I had scored some free food, but Angus and the group of boys he was with had seen me pick the pie up.

'You're not going to eat that are you?' they started. 'Are you poor or something? Tim, Tim, the rubbish bin.'

'I'm not going to eat it,' I smiled, feeling hot in the face.

'Then why did you pick it up?' one boy argued.

I just wanted them to leave me alone, so to avert their focus I put the pie on Angus's head and rubbed it in.

Afterwards I felt so bad I helped him wash the mince out of his hair. From that point on we were friends.

Angus had had a problem before meeting me. Kids were constantly picking on him. That changed when he started hanging out with me, the unhinged ninja guy. However, one student hadn't been deterred. Darren was younger, taller and bigger than Angus and was out to make his mark in the school. A junior student would look pretty cool after beating up a senior. Angus appeared an easy win. He wasn't a trouble-maker and he certainly wasn't a fighter.

Angus asked me for help, but the interactions between him and Darren always happened when I wasn't around. Angus wanted me to hunt Darren down at school and give him some ninja medicine. I wasn't keen.

At this point I was well aware that the school was looking for any excuse to kick me out, and I had no interest in proving myself tougher than other kids in the school, especially since most of them looked down on me.

So under my direction Angus and I broke up our normal routine around the school and worked on avoiding Darren. Angus was resistant, though, since he and a couple of others wanted to see me take the boy out.

One lunchtime I decided we should hang out in the school hall where there were lots of students sitting around in little groups. Even a male teacher was there, chatting with a bunch of girls. I figured we would be safe with all those witnesses, which included a member of the staff.

Darren and his mates were out looking for Angus and they found us. Angus looked at me. I knew he was scared. I tutted and sighed because I really didn't want to fight.

Angus stood to meet the threat front on. Darren towered over him, threatening to smash him. Angus tried to stick up for himself.

The hall was quiet. The other students and the teacher were all just sitting there, watching the drama unfold before them. No one was moving to intervene.

Resistant to fighting, I suddenly had an idea. I jumped to my feet and in a booming voice told Darren off as though I were an adult scolding a child.

'No!' I bellowed. 'This is not okay! Leave him alone! No one's fighting!'

Through my voice I took control, commanding the entire hall. It was as though time froze for that brief moment. Everyone was still and stunned, especially Darren. His face burnt red as I got in between him and Angus and continued to tell him off.

'You get out of here now!' I cried, stepping right up into his face. 'Go on!'

Darren responded like any teen being told off by an adult would. He grumbled under his breath as he marched off out of the hall. All eyes remained on me.

'See, I told you he was crazy,' one girl said.

I saw the teacher just sitting there, watching. Another teacher was peering through the door of the nearby office. They didn't praise me for preventing a fight or even try to address the issue. They were waiting for me to go off, but I wasn't going to play into their expectations. I wasn't going to give them a reason to kick me out of school.

Without saying another word, I sat back down. It was over.

Angus had wanted me to beat Darren up, but right now he and the other boys were quiet.

I sat there—angry at the school, angry at the teachers, the students, the world. They didn't intervene, yet they judged and condemned. They complained, yet few were ever willing to do anything to make things better.

At least Darren never messed with Angus again. In fact Darren became my friend. It turned out that after he'd cooled down he respected me for how I'd dealt with the situation. He became another person who would wave and call out my name.

I was certain my Primary School Teacher, Miss Foote would have been proud. I was developing quite a skill of addressing violent situations with non-violence.

¤ ¤ ¤

My friendship with Angus was intimate. We had both faced adversity and challenges in our lives and we found comfort in being with one another. Because men had often targeted me as a boy I had assumed I must be gay, and through my relationship with Angus I was able to explore that. Yet as close as I was to Angus he never told me that he had epilepsy.

His seizure happened on a day when I wasn't at school. Mum and Dad had me home for a week doing work around the property.

Angus was in the school library when the seizure came. A number of students pointed out afterwards that no one would have laughed if I'd been there. But I wasn't there, and as Angus convulsed on the floor, biting his tongue and wetting his pants, students stood around laughing at him.

Angus never went back to school after that. He couldn't face it. I got to see him one more time and then he headed south. A year later Angus was dead. He'd had an accident riding his motorbike.

I had protected Angus at high school, but I hadn't been there that day he'd had his epileptic seizure. He was a dear friend, and one I missed.

Years later his mum thanked me.

'I am so grateful that my son got to have a special relationship in his life,' she said, 'and that you were the one he had it with.'

I lost a number of mates during those years, and each of them were significant to me and my life. There were even two brothers, Bobby and Rueben, who died just months apart.

    I love and miss each and every one of them.

SCISSORS

People were now encouraging me to talk about what was going on at home. My friends, their mums, my aunties and the odd teacher were all telling me to 'Let it out, boy'. Meanwhile Mum, Dad and other relatives had always told me to keep my mouth shut. Only snitches and narks talked, and speaking out about the family was being disloyal.

However, things had escalated at home.

Katie was certain Mum had another man. Mum had always been promiscuous, but Katie believed that this time it was different—that it was a proper relationship.

Mum was rarely home, and when she was, she and Dad would argue.

In our two storeyed, A-framed house on Barr Road the dining area was open all the way up to the roof. Near the top were some lights which hadn't been working properly. One morning Dad decided he wanted to have a go at fixing them. He growled at me to get downstairs. Dad and I carried the ladder from the garage in through the house, and leaned it up against the wall in the dining area .

'You hold the ladder,' Dad said, which was really his way of saying, *If anything happens to me you're going to get a hiding.*

Height was a fear for Dad, but he was set on doing it so this was a tense time for both of us.

I went under the ladder and grasped both sides with my hands, holding it firmly.

Dad climbed towards the lights. I made the mistake of looking up. Often around the house Dad wore nothing but a small pair of shorts, and today was no exception.

I was quick to avert my eyes, which caused the ladder to shake a little.

'Are you holding the ladder?' Dad snapped from above.

'Yes,' I replied, making sure both of my hands were visible to him.

Behind Dad, Mum walked out of the kitchen, wiping her hands on a tea towel. She stood looking at me holding the ladder and then up at Dad fiddling with the lights. She gestured at me with her eyes and hands.

I frowned, showing I didn't understand what she was trying to say.

Mum made the gesture again, this time clearer—moving both hands out in a pushing action. 'Push the ladder,' she mouthed.

I smiled, thinking she was joking. However the expression on her face grew more serious.

'Push the ladder over,' she demanded, again demonstrating with her hands.

I shook my head. I knew full well what would happen if I pushed the ladder over. Dad would get hurt from the fall, and if he was able to get back up from it I'd be the one getting hurt next.

Mum persisted in trying to get me to push the ladder over. 'Do it,' she glared, while pointing a finger.

I shook my head again.

Dad felt the ladder shake. 'Oi!' he boomed from above. 'Are you holding the ladder?'

'Yes,' I nodded, making the mistake of looking up again.

Mum shook her head at me with disappointment, sighed, and went back into the kitchen.

¤ ¤ ¤

Dad's response to Mum's distance was to go all out on the booze. People were constantly at our house drinking and partying. It didn't matter if it was school the next day—the music would play loud all night long. Dad liked having one song on repeat. Often it was Joe Cocker singing '*I get by with a little help from my friends*,' or Van Morrison's '*Gloria*' going over and over. I would sneak downstairs sometime around 3am, when I was sure everyone was gone or asleep, and switch the music off.

At school I had little purpose or plan. I was well behind the other students and seemed to be constantly in trouble.

Michael and another mate were worried about me so they approached a teacher, who in turn encouraged me to see the school counsellor, Mr Jones. Since my college was only too quick to punish me, I thought maybe if I was up front about what was going on at home they might actually support me.

Mr Jones agreed to meet with me. Each session I would sit across from him in his small room and talk about home. Ten minutes into our third session Mr Jones stood up and lay down on the floor by my feet.

What's going on here? I thought to myself, crossing my arms and bringing my legs together.

'I like to lie down like this sometimes,' Mr Jones said. 'It helps me get things into perspective.'

I looked at the door.

Mr Jones tapped the floor beside him. 'Come and join me, Tim.'

'Nah, I'm all right,' I replied.

Mr Jones turned over and curled up into a ball. He started to shake and cry. 'My wife has left me,' he said. He beckoned for me to come and lie with him, to comfort him.

I stayed glued to my seat.

Mr Jones soon got up and I was allowed to leave.

In response to queries from people concerned about my welfare, Mum had long been in the habit of telling me there was nothing wrong with my life, and that any problems I had were just in my head. So I shrugged off my apprehensions about Mr Jones, telling myself I'd been reading too much into it, and returned to his office for my next session.

But now it was different. Mr Jones no longer had time to see me.

'Follow me, Tim,' he said.

He took me up to the school's administration block and into the office of the Deputy Principal.

'How can I help?' the DP asked.

'Tim's having some issues at home,' Mr Jones explained. 'Perhaps you could give his parents a call and sort it out over the phone?'

My heart dropped.

'That won't be a problem,' the DP said.

'So I can leave him with you?' Mr Jones queried.

'Yep, just leave it with me,' the DP replied.

Mr Jones walked away, and just like that I had been passed onto somebody else.

The DP picked up the phone. 'We'll have this sorted out in no time, Tim,' he said, dialling my home number.

I watched in horror. *Please be asleep, please be asleep*, I pleaded in my head.

Dad could sleep through anything, especially after a night of drinking. He sometimes liked to strip down to his underwear and sleep on the trampoline outside in the sun. He liked to get his complexion darker. I was hoping this was what Dad was doing right at this very moment, well out of earshot of the phone.

Don't pick up, please don't pick up.

Thankfully Dad didn't answer the Deputy Principal's call. If he had I would have gotten a hiding when I got home, and I was even more scared of Mum's reaction than Dad's. The school clearly had no idea what I was dealing with at home and what my life was like.

After the failed call no other support was offered by the school. I was simply expected to fit in and carry on like all the other students. But I couldn't. I was on a collision course and there was just no stopping it.

¤ ¤ ¤

It was a stupid thing to do, and it was exactly the opportunity the college had been waiting for. One day I found a pair of scissors left in a classroom. I took out the screw and separated the scissors into two pieces. Walking outside, I threw one half of the scissors over the school buildings into a nearby empty paddock.

A student tried to stop me from throwing the remaining half. 'Don't do it,' he said. 'It's dangerous. You could hurt someone.'

Being reckless was the only thing I had over the other kids and I was sick of people looking down at me so I ignored the student and threw it. The throw wasn't the best and with the wind it flew in a little, towards the school but then it seemed to clear. I walked off, thinking nothing more of it.

Sometime later the bell rang calling for a special assembly on the school court. Special assemblies were only called when a student or students had severely broken a school rule.

As I made my way through the crowd I passed my sister. 'Hey, Katie,' I said. 'This is the first special assembly that doesn't have anything to do with me.'

She laughed, knowing that the previous special assemblies had all been to do with me and something that I had done.

Rather than sit on the asphalt with the rest of my class I sat on a nearby railing and gazed over the crowd, wondering who was in trouble this time. I was sitting tall and proud because I knew I was clean. I had been trying hard to behave and hadn't done anything wrong. I wasn't going to give the school any reason to kick me out.

The principal appeared on a step overlooking the students and staff. He was not a happy man.

'Boy, someone's in trouble,' I heard a kid say.

Everyone quietened down.

The principal peered out over the students. 'Does anyone have any information on who threw this!' he boomed, holding up one half of a pair of scissors.

As soon as I saw it I burst out laughing. I laughed so loud the principal stopped and, along with everybody else, looked directly at me. Katie was mouthing at me to stop laughing because I was giving myself away, but I knew it was over. My schooling had come to an end.

The second piece of the scissors hadn't landed in the empty paddock. Apparently it had smashed through a classroom window and stabbed into a desk near a teacher. The teacher thought someone was out to kill him.

I had given the school the very excuse they'd been waiting for. I was out.

Following the assembly, I found Mr Jones. I confessed to the scissors in the hope that maybe now the school would take my request for help seriously.

I was suspended first, and then on returning to school was told I could finish the last few weeks of the term off and then I wasn't to return. They kicked me out.

The school had known about my home life, but they had no idea how to address it—and more importantly, had no interest in trying. They would say it themselves: 'We're teachers, not social workers.'

When I was kicked out of college I still couldn't recite the alphabet from A to Z. I didn't know my times tables and I couldn't tell the time on analogue clocks. Rather than address my learning shortfalls, my high school had instead plonked me in little rooms with worksheets or pushed me to the backs of classrooms. Many of my college teachers were open with the fact that they saw me as a lost cause. The school had set me up to fail just as my family had, and I failed fantastically. I played my part perfectly. With a pair of scissors I severed my schooling. It was so predictable it was laughable.

For a long time I believed I had failed school. However people in education, whom I came to know as an adult, would stress that it was the school that had failed me.

¤ ¤ ¤

A few years later Mr Jones, the school counsellor, fled the country after getting a female student at the college pregnant.

FISH AND CHIPS ON THE BEACH

Mum was on the move.

Katie saw it coming before anybody else did, but even she didn't know the full extent.

With a pair of scissors I had given my high school the excuse it needed to kick me out. Yet the scissors not only severed my schooling, they also brought an end to my home life. Mum now had the excuse she'd been waiting for, and with Uncle Todd's help her plan was set to play out.

I was sent to live with my newly married cousin, Josie, and to work on building sites with her husband in Orewa.

To start work I required my birth certificate. When I asked Mum for it she gave me one I hadn't seen before. It named Peter as my father and gave me his last name. Peter was a convicted rapist of women and children.

I asked Mum for my official certificate—the one that said that I was a Tipene. It was the only birth certificate I'd ever known.

'That's your only birth certificate.' Mum gestured at the document in my hand. 'That's the one you use.'

I was confused. I was certain there was another one. I had seen it, hadn't I?

I waited till the afternoon when I was home alone, then went into Mum's room and searched through her papers. I found adoption papers for me dated 7th December 1979, with Mum and Dad named as the adopters. I also found my birth certificate stating that Mum and Dad were my legal parents, and that my last name was Tipene.

Mum didn't want me using the name Tipene anymore.

I remembered Nana and Poppa Tipene, and how proud they had been to call me their grandson. I had grown up with the name Tipene. That's who I was. I took the documents, thinking they might disappear if I didn't.

¤ ¤ ¤

I knew that I wasn't a builder. I tried and worked hard in Orewa, but it just wasn't happening. My cousin Josie and her husband were newly married so it was certainly a case of threes a crowd. I spent most evenings walking the beach just to give them space. I would sit on the sand and write. At least at school there were people that I had known who I could talk to. Here I didn't know anyone, and I was being forced down a career path that wasn't of my own choosing.

After a couple of months of living and working in Orewa I got a phone call.

It was Mum. I hadn't heard from any of my family so I was surprised to hear from her.

Mum told me she was coming to visit me, and that we would have fish and chips together on the beach. Just her and me. I was surprised and excited. For once in my life I was going to get to spend some quality time with my mother.

Mum picked me up on Sunday afternoon and drove us around to Red Beach. I was so happy to see her. Mum pulled up at some shops, gave me some cash and sent me in to get the takeaways. She wasn't having any food herself because she said she wasn't feeling hungry. Mum then drove us to the beach.

When we got there Mum told me she was going to visit a friend up the road and that I could eat my fish and chips on the beach while I waited for her. Mum said she wouldn't be long and we could have time together when she returned.

It turned out that I was once again Mum's cover story. While I sat there all afternoon waiting for her, Mum was having dinner with her new man, George. By the time Mum came back to the beach it was well into the evening and she had to get home because she had work the next day. She dropped me off in Orewa.

When Mum got pregnant I was the last to know, however, Katie was with Mum in the hospital for the birth.

Katie thought the baby was looking pretty white. 'It doesn't look like Dad,' she said.

'That's because Dad isn't the father,' Mum replied.

Katie wasn't surprised, but she still felt hurt.

I had never been privy to what was going on in our family so I don't know when Dad found out. I did hear that it was pretty messy though. Mum and Dad separated.

Another baby arrived a couple of years later. It was a girl this time. George was the father of both the children, and an active father, yet Mum gave the children Dad's last name, calling them Donny Tipene and Clara Tipene.

Mum took it even further by having Donny and Clara call their father, 'George', and Dad, 'Dad'.

Dad had chosen to be powerless in life. He had allowed Mum to dominate and manipulate him. With George it was no different. Mum had George chasing her and his children all over the country. He could only visit when Mum felt like it.

¤ ¤ ¤

My time with Josie came to an end. The married couple were having issues so I was sent to Hamilton. I ended up sleeping in my cousin, Megan's, lounge and paying half her rent.

I appreciated my Uncle Todd and my cousins attempts to set me up with a job; however I was too inhibited by the trauma and complexity of my childhood abuse to take full advantage of their help My relatives couldn't understand this though. They just assumed I was lazy, irresponsible and unappreciative.

They were well and truly over me by this stage anyway. Uncle Todd had always been on his own with my five cousins, and he and Mum had a weird relationship. It was as though he was besotted with her. Uncle Todd did a lot for Mum and was always willing to help her out.

When I was small, every Christmas holidays us kids were sent to stay with Uncle Todd at his bach. I was grateful to my uncle and cousins for taking us in. They certainly gave us a taste of how the rich live and Leigh was an amazing place to be for the holidays. Fishing, swimming, water sports and more extended family.

As kind as my uncle and cousins were, when I got older I became aware that I was a burden for them. It was as if my uncle had been taking me, the difficult, troublesome boy, off my mother's hands for a while so she could have a break.

One afternoon my cousin, Daniel, and his mate started an impromptu wrestling match with me in his bedroom. I was a young teen at the time and we were in one of the many flash homes in Hamilton that Uncle Todd had owned over the years. Daniel lifted me up straight into the path of the fast-spinning ceiling fan.

Whack!

The fan hit me in the top of the head.

With blood going everywhere, I was left holding the gash while Uncle Todd raced around in a panic, trying to save his expensive carpet.

'Get him off the carpet!' Uncle Todd yelled at my cousins as he tried to catch the blood with old towels.

Daniel gave me a towel to hold onto my wound.

'Don't give him that,' Uncle Todd directed. 'Get him a rag!'

My cousins whisked me downstairs and out of the house. Katie and I were left standing outside, trying to control the flow of blood from my head as we waited for Daniel to take me to A&E. The wound wasn't hurting, but I was scared.

'Can you see my brains?' I asked Katie, bowing my head so that she could look.

'I can't see anything,' she replied. 'Just blood.'

'I don't want to die,' I said.

'You're not going to die, Timmy.' Katie laughed nervously.

Daniel and his mate finally appeared, and they dropped me off at a clinic. People were horrified at the sight of the blood all over my face and head when I walked through the door.

'I think I need to see someone,' I said to the lady at reception.

I ended up with a shaved head and stitches.

Now I'd been kicked out of school Uncle Todd was trying hard to help

Mum by sorting out her good-for-nothing son. When he later met a girlfriend of mine, Uncle Todd told me that she was too good for me, and that summed up his opinion of me.

My relatives lost patience with me on the building site in Hamilton. I just wasn't cutting it. So Uncle Todd passed me over to a painting firm.

Battling my past, I ended up isolated and alone in Hamilton. My self-loathing was at an all-time high and I took to self-harming—cutting myself with a knife and burning matches into the inside of my forearms. I made two lines of burn marks up each arm. Thoughts of suicide were my only companion, yet I didn't want to die. I turned to promiscuous behaviour, yet that only made it worse. After each sexual encounter I felt so guilty and ashamed that I cut and burned myself even more.

I didn't know anyone in Hamilton other than my rich cousins, and things were only getting worse with them. Greg even tried to beat me up in the middle of Queen Street.

It was over a dispute that I was having with his sister, Megan. Megan had lost the money that I'd paid her for my share of the monthly bills. She wanted me to pay the money again. I couldn't afford to, and as far as I was concerned it was Megan's responsibility to cover the money she'd lost. Megan didn't agree. Greg was thinking that a good hiding would bring me around to Megan's way of thinking.

My boss at the painting firm thought the same thing. Mr Smythe was infatuated with model-like Megan, so before giving me my next wages he paid her a visit, took money directly out of my pay packet and handed it to her. When Mr Smythe arrived on the job he boasted proudly about what he'd done while handing me what remained of my wages. He then raised his fists and took a boxing posture in front of me. He said that if I had a problem with it then he would be happy to teach me a lesson right there and then.

Mr Smythe was a dodgy character. Most of the workers he hired were on the run from the law. Mr Smythe made out that he was helping them and that it was an act of Christian kindness. The workers thought otherwise. In reality Mr Smythe had built up a cheap labour force that he could pay low wages to under the table.

Every now and then a workmate's picture would end up on Crime Watch on television, with police asking the public for any information on their whereabouts. That would be the last time I ever saw that workmate.

After Mr Smythe had threatened me I walked off the job. I packed up my things and returned to Auckland. I temporarily moved in with my mate Michael at his brother's place up in Helensville. I was homeless and unemployed, but at least I was back in the Kaipara with people I knew.

CONTRADICTING INFLUENCES

When I was 10 my family had a holiday in Rotorua. While we were there we attended the local chapter of our church. The church was well connected throughout the country and people in Rotorua knew of our family. After the service a family invited us to their home for dinner.

As soon as I walked in the door of the house the woman of the family took an interest in me. She kept smiling warmly and talking, not to my siblings, but to me. It appeared to be in direct opposition to Mum. Perhaps she had heard something.

The family we were visiting had a toddler. During our visit I got down on the floor and started playing with the toddler's little Tomy train set in the corner while the toddler slept in another room. Mum wasn't happy. She made a remark about me being too old to play with trains.

The woman responded by saying how quietly I played and that I was obviously used to being on my own. It was an observation as much as a compliment.

I tipped the basket of toys over so I could find more train track. Mum said I was making a mess. Hearing this, the woman of the house left the room and shortly afterwards returned with a large container of track for the train set.

'Here you go, Tim,' she said. 'Now I want to see you cover the whole floor of the lounge with a track for the train.'

I was amazed, and in love.

For dessert the woman dished out her own home-made coffee ice cream. It was the best ice cream I had ever tasted. Coffee became my new favourite flavour.

I wanted to know if there was any left. Mum said I wasn't to have any more.

The woman went into the kitchen and reappeared with a bowl. 'Tim, there is some ice cream left,' she said. 'It would be a big help if you could finish it up for me.'

There was heaps left, and with such an important task I couldn't let the woman down. Mum was powerless to stop me.

After dinner I went back to building the train set. As I sat there on the carpet I wondered if the woman and her family would mind me living with them. The woman was so kind and caring that I figured my family could just leave me here. I was certain that under the right circumstances Mum and Dad would be happy to palm me off.

I didn't get to entertain the idea for very long. Mum was keen to leave.

When we drove away Mum was quiet. A little way down the road, though, she went into a bitching session about the woman and her family. It seemed to be an attack on me as much as the woman.

We were only with that woman and her family for a short time. I don't even remember her name, yet in just few hours she impacted my entire life.

Every now and then adults like her would turn up in my life and contradict what Mum and Dad said about me, and what I had been led to believe about myself. That woman made me feel I was someone good, and someone worthy of love. It was a wonderful gift. From then on I could never go past a train set or the taste of coffee.

¤ ¤ ¤

Stan was a preacher in my church, a good man who practised what he preached. He was one of only a few adults who ever took any real interest in me and in my life. I didn't get to see him much, but when I did the two of us would spend hours talking. He listened to me. He believed in me. He was one of my angels.

Stan gifted me a *Bible* when I was twelve. It was just prior to Mum pulling away from the church. Mum was all clear of her cancer by then so she didn't need the church anymore. Or perhaps the charade was crumbling and people were starting to see what was really going on in our home. Regardless, it was back to parties, alcohol and drugs for her.

On the inside of the *Bible* cover Stan wrote:

Have the courage to stand when it is easier to sit

Have the courage to speak when it is easier to be silent

Have the courage to go on when it is easier to go back

These words became my mantra and my guide for living life.

A few months later at school we studied Mohandas K. Gandhi in Social Studies. I quickly saw that Gandhi was someone who had been a living embodiment of the words Stan had written to me, someone who had put those words into practice. My study into the life of Gandhi became a significant moment in my life. My eyes were opened. I was looking around at everybody else in my class to see if they were seeing it too. Here was someone who had lived truth.

In church, in schools, in the community, on TV and in music that we listened to there was so much talk about doing what was right and living truthfully, yet I noticed there were very few actually practising it. Adults were good at preaching, good at getting emotional and carried away with ideals, good at praising Jesus, but few of them were actually living truthfully. Instead most people were wrapped up in their own lives, thinking about what fashionable items they were going to buy or where they were going to spend their next holiday. Even the majority of those pushing causes weren't living truthfully.

At 14 my life was a lie, a charade. So many knew about the ongoing dysfunction in my home. They knew about the abuse and violence—it was the shadow in every room—yet it remained unsaid. Family, friends of my parents and people in the community kept up a pretence that all was fine in the world. It was a charade that protected my parents, and those who knew about it, from having to face the truth. I felt dirty and unclean from being a central part of such a lie.

Rather than own, accept and address the abuse that had happened to them as children, Mum and Dad had both chosen to ignore it, put on a brave face, soldier on and struggle through life. Yet their unresolved hurt and pain continuously seeped out, causing even more destruction and suffering, and perpetuating a never-ending cycle of further violence and abuse.

I had come to know the cycle of violence well, and how one act determined another. I had been raised on violence and abuse—it was the culture of my family.

So I was impressed by Gandhi and his stand for non-violence, and by how much he and his supporters managed to achieve through it. Gandhi spoke of the greys in life. He wasn't into the absolutes — black and white, good and bad, villains and victims — that society tends to cling to. Gandhi freed himself of hatred towards his oppressors. He was out for the betterment of all mankind. At the time I was learning martial arts and looking to idols like Bruce Lee and Chuck Norris. I was wrapped up in the 80s ninja boom. But life wasn't an action movie full of bad people and good people. Everyone has their story of how they came to be who they are and why they make the choices that they do.

Mum and Dad could be incredibly cruel and abusive to me, yet they weren't monsters. They were both damaged individuals who were living out their hurt and shame.

Since I was by nature a caring and considerate person, non-violence looked to me to be a viable option.

I took on the belief that violent situations could be addressed in non-violent ways. To overcome Dad beating me I didn't necessarily have to beat him. There were other ways.

Gandhi's life and work inspired me. It reminded me of how Miss Foote didn't like fighting and how I had curbed my impulse to fight since knowing her. It took me back to the cloakroom where I showed Mrs Battersby the lump in the pit of my arm after Dad punched me. Her tearful reaction and hug had brought a voice to life within me—a voice that said the abuse wasn't right. And that voice had never gone away.

Reading about Gandhi brought to mind the love and acceptance of my whānau, whom I hadn't seen in years, and the love and generosity of Sakapo, the Fijian who'd taught me to carve.

The fire within me was burning bright. I was going to live a truthful life.

I wasn't going to hide from the shadows. Mum and Dad's lie wasn't mine to keep.

My nature to question and challenge had been affirmed. I was going to stand up, speak up and go on. I wasn't going to settle for less than that.

The martial arts were teaching me self-control and to be brave. I would use that to be non-violent. Ever since I was little I had been telling myself that I wouldn't grow up to be like Mum and Dad. That I wouldn't live their life. Gandhi showed me that one person could make a difference, and this was exactly what I was going to do.

¤ ¤ ¤

Mr Manukau was our school bus driver. He was an old Māori man who always dressed nicely with a buttoned-up shirt, pants and a 1930s-style hat. He would pick us kids up each morning and take us to school, then deliver us home in the afternoon. No one mucked about on Mr Manukau's ride. If anyone did he'd threaten to smack them with the brush he used to clean the bus.

'I'll give you bloody kids a hiding!' he'd yell, holding the brush up.

Everyone would quieten down.

I never saw Mr Manukau hit anyone though. However from time to time he did stop the bus and tell kids to get off, making them walk the rest of the way home. I was made to walk a couple of times. It didn't matter that I hadn't done anything wrong—I was just in the vicinity of those who had.

One afternoon Mr Manukau asked Shaun and me about our last name.

'You're Tipene?' he queried.

'Yes,' Shaun said.

'What is your father's name?' he asked.

I told him.

'Do you know where you guys come from?' Mr Manukau asked further. 'Do you know your marae or iwi?'

Shaun and I looked at each other.

'Nga Puhi,' I said, since that was what Dad had said.

'I think we're related,' Mr Manukau announced.

From then on Mr Manukau took a special interest in me. He would get me to stay on the bus and finish the route with him, and he'd drop me off on the way back. He liked me to sit up the front and talk with him. He would tell me about his family, about his time in the army. He mentioned that he'd been in World War 2, but he didn't like to talk about that.

One day Mr Manukau got me to take a book home. It was a book that he had put together himself, detailing his whakapapa. It showed that we were related. Mr Manukau wanted me to show it to Dad. Dad wasn't interested. I didn't tell Mr Manukau that.

Sometimes when it was just Mr Manukau and me on the bus, he would park on the side of the road and take me into fields and the bush, showing me trees and plants that were used in rongoā—Māori medicine. I helped him collect flowers to make soap.

With my neighbours, Heta and Mary, and now Mr Manukau, it was clear that Māoridom wasn't finished with me. The interest, time and effort that these elders put into me showed that there was a lot more to me than what my parents saw. The elders showed me that I was someone worth investing in, just as my whānau had in the early years of my life. They made me feel I had something to offer.

CHOICE

I stood on the side of the road with my thumb out, looking for a ride. I was eighteen, back living at home to look after Katie and I was heading from Helensville to West Auckland. Hitchhiking had become my main mode of transport. I didn't have a driver's license and didn't feel confident behind the wheel. I got to meet a lot of nice people through hitchhiking. Met some interesting ones too.

A man pulled up in an old Holden. I got in the front passenger seat and we headed off. The friendly driver and I talked a bit and in the moments where there was silence I looked out the window, but my attention wasn't on the scenery going by. I was wrestling with my conscience.

In the bag on my lap I had a towel, and wrapped up in that towel was a large amount of cannabis—heads and cabbage all mixed together. At 15 I had made the decision not to drink alcohol or do drugs and I had stuck to it. I was taking the cannabis to an uncle who was looking to sell it to workmates. My friend Bobby had come across the marijuana plants growing among a patch of mānuka. It was clearly someone's patch, but Bobby wanted me to help him raid it. And now here I was, sitting in a car, on my way to take the drugs to an uncle.

I was at a crossroads in my life and had a choice to make.

Prior to this trip I had been offered a large sum of money to hurt some guy in town. Those requesting the payback were waiting for my reply as to whether or not I would sort out this man who had wronged them.

The police had also been turning up at home to question me about crimes that had taken place in the community.

'Don't bring your trouble round here!' Dad would yell.

The police knew what had been going on in my home when I was growing up. A couple of years earlier I had even asked a sergeant for help. He and his wife attended the same church as me and my family, and one summer he was responsible for a small community up north. My family and I just happened be staying at the same place. The sergeant was frustrated with a recent bout of vandalism in the community and was trying to catch the person responsible.

At a church barbecue I grabbed an opportunity to be alone with him.

'I hear you're trying to catch the person who's been vandalising the neighbourhood,' I said.

'It's only a matter of time,' the sergeant replied.

'It's me,' I said.

He frowned. 'Why would you do something like that, Tim?'

I told him about the violence and abuse at home. I was thinking that surely a sergeant in the police force could help me, surely he could intervene, especially since he knew Mum and Dad, and went to the same church. I told him that I was angry—angry that my family were treating me this way, and angry that so many people knew about the violence and abuse, yet nobody would do anything about it.

The sergeant thought for a moment. Then he turned to me. 'Don't let me catch you doing it,' he said.

I watched him walk away.

He never spoke to my parents. There was no intervention.

Aunties had encouraged me to talk about what was going on at home. However I was quickly learning that it didn't matter how many people I talked to, I was still on my own with the violence and abuse. No one was going to help me.

A short while after I had spoken to the sergeant the local police at home became very interested in me. I was even called into the station for a chat.

The sergeant who interviewed me started off by saying that he was well aware that there had been issues at home. He said that he wanted to help and support me with those issues, but first I would have to help myself by helping him.

There had been a number of petty crimes in the neighbourhood and he believed I was responsible. In order to receive help all I had to do was confess to those crimes.

'We know you did it, Tim,' the sergeant said. 'We just want to hear it from you.' He kept saying, 'We're here to help you, Tim. We're on your side.'

Alarm bells started ringing in my head. I was being stitched up. The police had no intention of helping me. They could have intervened in my family years ago. The fact was, some of the local police drank at the pub with Dad, and Dad was popular in the community. At one stage he was even crowned Miss Kaukapakapa at the local pub two or three years in a row, for dressing up as Tina Turner and lip-syncing her songs while performing on stage.

It was easier for the police to convict a teenager and lock him up than it was to address the ongoing abuse and mistreatment that had led to the teenager acting out in the first place. The police were trying to pin a whole list of crimes on me, the majority of which I had no knowledge of. I was an easy target. The more the sergeant sided up to me, telling me he had my back and wanted to help me, the more I could see I was being led down a path of no return. The sergeant was wanting to put me away. I knew that if I ended up in a correction facility I would be worse off. I'd end up just like my father.

'I don't know anything,' I said.

'Uh, c'mon, Tim,' the sergeant replied. 'Let me help you.'

I shook my head. 'I don't know anything,' I repeated.

Now I was in a Holden on my way to deliver drugs to my uncle. I didn't want to let him down—I wanted his approval—but was this to be my future? The path of crime was stretched out before me. It had always been expected that I would go that way and I felt as though everything was stacked against me being good. There were few who believed in me.

But I didn't want the police coming around looking for me all the time. I didn't want to go to prison like my biological father. I didn't want to have to look over my shoulder every day because someone was out to get me after

I'd raided their drug patch or hurt someone connected to them. I wanted a good life. I wanted to be someone who made a difference—to be the hero I had hungered for as a kid. I wanted a wife and children, a family of my own with a nice home.

Could I go against the grain? Take the harder, lonely path of being my own man, stand on my own two feet, and determine who I was going to be? Be a light in this world, rather than a shadow?

These thoughts were racing around in my head.

I turned to my driver. 'Do you smoke?' I asked.

He looked at me. 'Yeah,' he said.

'Do you smoke the good stuff?' I queried.

The man laughed. 'Uh, yeah, bro.'

'I've got something you might want,' I said.

'Uh, yeah?'

I reached into my bag, pulled out the towel and carefully unwrapped it on the bench seat between us, making sure not to lose any of its contents.

The man's eyes grew at the large amount of weed.

'Do you want it?' I asked, feeling bad about offering it to him. I didn't want others to have to take on my burden.

'Yeah, I'll take some,' he beamed.

'You can have all of it if you want,' I said.

'Eh?' the man stuttered, looking amazed.

'I don't want it,' I told him. 'Sorry, I probably should throw it away.'

'Nah, nah, nah, don't do that!' the man gasped. 'I'll take it.'

'Sorry, it's all mixed together,' I said.

'Nah, nah, it's all good,' the man replied.

He wanted to know why I was getting rid of the weed so I explained to him that I didn't want to go down this path. That it wasn't the right direction for me.

'Uh, good on you, boy,' the driver nodded. Then he smiled at me. 'I'll take you where every you want to go, bro.'

We both laughed.

As I looked out the window again, I was aware that I felt a lot lighter, as though a dark cloud had lifted off me. I was free. I felt that my future was finally mine, and not some preordained path I had no choice in.

My driver couldn't believe his luck, yet I felt bad about giving the illegal drug to him. He kept thanking me right up till when I got out of his car. This just made me more embarrassed. The man waved and tooted as he drove away.

My uncle never asked about the drugs. I guessed that he just assumed I hadn't come through as usual. I didn't care. I had decided there would be no more drugs, no more police, and no more looking over my shoulder. I knew that if I wanted to sort out my life I had a mountain ahead of me, but on this day I felt I had made a good step.

MT TABOR

Since being kicked out of home and school I'd been going from job to job, home to home and relationship to relationship. Having just being laid off from yet another job, I'd ended up on the benefit and living out of my $200 car.

My mate Michael found out I was homeless again and talked me into squatting in a rundown shack that he knew of out at a beach at South Head on the Kaipara Harbour. I appreciated Michael's help.

The shack was set amongst some trees. Michael helped me clean it up. Only a couple of the windows were still intact,
; the rest had sheets of plywood pushed into them to cover them up. I would push the plywood out when the weather was good to let some fresh air in.

There was a crude sink and tap which gave me running water from a small corrugated tank outside. There was no toilet and no power, so I lived by candlelight and as the beach was only a ten-minute walk away I would use the public toilet there. There was even a shower on the outside of the toilet block. This is where I would shower in my shorts with soap and shampoo, much to the amusement of some of the locals.

The shack was right next to the main road and the public phone box. When people used the phone it was hard not to hear their business. I was excited one evening when the phone rang. I ran outside and answered it. The caller was able to tell me the number she'd phoned and from that point on I had a phone line people could reach me on, which I needed for prospective job interviews.

After a few days of staying at the shack, though, I got sick with chickenpox. I had caught them off a friend and was laid up for days on my own. It wasn't a good time because it showed up just how alone I was in the world. By the end of it I was at an all-time low.

In an act of self-loathing and hate, I made a fire.

I now felt so bad about who I was that I took all the things that represented me and burnt them. I sought to rid myself of the very essence that made me, me. I wanted to put an end to the person Mum had never been able to love. Then I could be someone else—someone new. A better, more ideal and more acceptable person for society.

¤ ¤ ¤

A few days later I came home and found the door to the shack kicked in. A note was nailed to the wall. It was from the owner. He was demanding that I phone him. Michael had warned me that the owner wasn't a nice guy and that I should avoid him at all costs. I packed up my bedding and clothes, and anything else I hadn't destroyed in the fire, and got out of there. I was back to staying with friends when I could, and the rest of the time sleeping in my car.

I had been scouring the local paper in search of another job. I hated being on the unemployment benefit and was constantly looking for ways to get off it. I didn't like the way social welfare looked down on me, berating me for failing to find a job, and I didn't like the stigma involved in being a beneficiary. I had found an advertisement for a live-in support person looking after adults with special needs at a place called Mt Tabor.

That would solve everything, I thought to myself. *I wouldn't need the benefit. I would have a job and a place to live.*

I applied for the position. On the day of the interview I dressed up in my cheap suit that I had left over from my church days. It was the suit I used for all my job interviews.

Mt Tabor was a charitable trust that provided homes and care for adults with special needs. The job I was going for was based at their residential farm in Kaukapakapa. When I walked up the path for the interview a short, bald man with Down's syndrome came out of the house. He ran, jumped up and wrapped his arms and legs around me and gave me a big, wet toothless kiss.

'This is Roger,' a staff member informed me as she appeared from the house.

Bewildered by my welcome, I was led inside. The people were nice and I enjoyed the interview. It was the most relaxed and informal I'd ever had.

I was asked when I could start.

'Straight away,' I said, knowing I had nowhere to live.

I was given a two-week trial. I moved in and fell in love with the job straight away. I was only 18, but I had found my place. Caring and looking after others. The pay was low, but I didn't care.

The adults with special needs were wonderful. I felt so blessed to be with them, and was quick to develop special relationships with each person.

I had gone into the job with the intention of changing the people and making their lives better. However Roger quickly showed me that there was nothing wrong with him or the others at Mt Tabor. It was me who needed changing.

My two-week trial ended on the night of a celebration. I had been anxious all day because I was desperate—I had nowhere else to go from here. Many of my friends had died and I feared I was heading the same way. I didn't feel qualified enough to keep the job, but I knew I needed it.

Throwing all embarrassment and shame aside, I collapsed on my knees in front of everyone and pleaded in tears to the manager to let me have the job.

'You already have it, Tim,' the manager replied. 'You had the job when you first walked in. Roger ran up to you, wrapped his arms and legs around you and gave you a big juicy kiss, and you didn't run away. People tend to run at that point, Tim.'

Relieved, I could finally breathe. Not only had I secured a job and a place to live, but now I also had a direction in life. I felt saved. I ended up staying at Mt Tabor for two years.

Roger had chosen me with his wet sloppy kiss and I am forever grateful. The two of us became inseparable. We became brothers. He even referred to Mum as his mum. This came about because I would phone Mum, and Roger wanted to know who I was talking to.

'I'm talking to my mum,' I said.

'Mum?' Roger would clarify.

'Yeah, Mum,' I replied.

Over time the term 'my' was dropped and it was just Mum, and Roger was keen to have a mum. When Roger was born his parents had disowned him, and he'd grown up in institutions. His teeth had been removed from an early age so he couldn't bite staff. As an adult he had been rescued by the good people of Mt Tabor.

Roger loved the idea of having family, of having me for a brother and of having a mum.

I hadn't given up pursuing Mum's love and acceptance, and periodically travelled down to Gisborne to see her. It was never good. I never felt welcome, yet I was desperate to win her over. On one such trip I took Roger with me.

On the way down I stopped so that Roger could use the toilet and I got him his favourite McDonald's Happy Meal. Forty minutes back into our trip and Roger wanted to go to the toilet again. We passed shops, but there were no toilets.

'Just hold on, Rogg,' I said. 'I'll find you a toilet.'

It got to the point where Roger couldn't hold on any longer. I pulled over to the side of the road and pointed at some small trees.

'Go behind those trees,' I said. 'You're just doing a wee, right, Rogg?'

Roger got out of the car, shook his head at the trees, and instead walked out into an open space and in plain sight dropped his pants and proceeded to do a number 2.

Shocked, I started looking around. A truck was approaching so I slid down in my seat to hide. As the truck roared passed it tooted at Roger.

'Oi, cut that out,' Roger said.

I had told Mum that I was bringing Roger down with me, and that we were staying for the weekend, but when we arrived there was nothing for us. Mum put Roger and me in a tiny room with only a mat to sleep on.

Still new to the job, I wasn't sure what the procedure was for sharing a bed with someone I was supposed to be looking after. While I was contemplating what to do Roger removed all of his clothes, jumped into bed, pulled back the covers revealing his nakedness and patted the mat for me to join him.

'C'mon,' he said.

I froze. 'Where're your pyjamas, Roger?' I asked.

'C'mon,' he said again. I now knew that Roger didn't wear pyjamas.

Keeping my clothes on, I got into bed. I turned away from Roger and curled up tight.

Roger cuddled in close. Leaning over, he gave me one of his sloppy kisses on the cheek and rubbed my head with his hand. 'Goodnight,' he muttered, as if talking to a baby.

Roger was an affectionate man, but there was never anything sexual in his behaviour. As uncomfortable as I felt, having been sexually abused as a child, I knew I was safe with him.

Mum kept her distance from Roger, yet she was happy to have him there because he proved to be great for her public relations in her position as bank manager of a local bank. Mum showed Roger off all about town, demonstrating that she was a community minded, caring businesswoman. Just like the many animals over the years, Roger had become a showpiece.

Roger couldn't care less. He just liked the idea of having a mum, he was never one to judge. I took him into a shop once and he came out with a new colouring book. Roger was so proud of his book that he wanted to show it off. He walked into the middle of a group of patched gang members, right there on the street, hugged the biggest one and showed him his new colouring book.

Startled and unsure, the gang member looked down at the small, bald, toothless man holding onto him. 'Uh, that's nice, eh?' he smiled.

THE ART OF SELF SABOTAGE

My role as support person at Mt Tabor was conditional. In order to remain in the position I had to commit to ongoing training at the Unitec Institute of Technology. I enjoyed the training because it was working on ourselves as much as learning how to work with others. It covered papers on human development, psychology, basic counselling and so on.

I couldn't believe my luck. I had a job, an income, a place to live, and was now being given tertiary education. I had hit the jackpot.

However I was starting to spiral out of control.

Mt Tabor was a safe place. It was a family atmosphere that did not accept abuse or violence, and I couldn't handle it. Every day I was riddled with anxiety and fear.

Not knowing what to do, I phoned Mum. I told her I was having nightmares and couldn't stop thinking about what had happened to me in the past.

'It's all in your head,' Mum said. 'There was nothing wrong with your past. Your life was normal, just like everybody else's.'

A week later Mum phoned me back to say she had spoken to her old doctor in Auckland about me and that she had good news. She said that she and the doctor were both convinced that I was bipolar, and that I needed to book an appointment with him so he could get me started on the medication. Mum went on to say that it explained why I had always been so different from her and the rest of the family. She said that once I was on the medication I would feel a whole lot better.

This worried me. At Mt Tabor I was working with adults with bipolar. I knew how strong their medication was.

Around about the same time, an older student on my course at Unitec had noticed I was struggling and offered to talk to me. Ray was a man who had completed training in counselling.

I went to his house one afternoon and he got me to open up. However I only got to say a little about my past before Ray stopped me.

'Whoa, that's enough, Tim,' he said.

'Uh, so it is nothing,' I replied, thinking, *Mum was right*.

'No, no,' Ray frowned. 'It's just that what you're describing is beyond my capabilities. I don't feel I'm qualified enough to work with what you're saying.'

'My mother tells me it's all in my head,' I explained.

Ray laughed. 'I bet she does.'

Ray suggested I talk to Roxy, our course tutor for counselling.

Mum kept phoning, trying to get me to commit to meeting her doctor so he could get me started on medication. I had never heard from her so much.

A few days after speaking to Ray I visited Roxy at her home. We sat down and I opened up about my past. After about thirty minutes of me talking Roxy put up her hands.

'I'm sorry, Tim,' she said, 'but this is beyond me.'

'What? So, you think I've got something to be upset about?' I queried.

Roxy looked at me. 'Tim, in all my years I've never worked with anyone with a story as bad as yours,' she answered. 'What you have explained to me is very traumatic. You have a huge amount of unpacking to do.'

Like Ray, Roxy didn't feel qualified to work with me. While it was disappointing, it was also a relief. The fact that the level of trauma I'd experienced was beyond their capabilities affirmed my experience. It was the best gift Ray and Roxy could have given me because it showed me that it wasn't all in my head. Roxy referred me to a service in west Auckland called Henderson House.

There was a year-long waiting list to get seen by a therapist at Henderson House, unless you were considered to be a threat to yourself and/or a threat to others. I was seen within a week.

My psychotherapist was Glenn and he was quick to knock Mum's diagnosis on the head.

'You are not bipolar and you do not require medication,' he said. 'That diagnosis would serve your mother, but it won't serve you.'

Each session of therapy with Glenn was intense and I was spinning from one to week to the next. I was highly anxious, feeling emotionally hurt and drained, and physically sick, yet I was so excited. Finally I was getting the help I had always sought.

Glenn was able to hear all about my past and be straight up and honest with me. He showed me the parts of my life that I was responsible for, and the abuse, violence and projections that were never my responsibility. I was learning how to parent myself and how to love myself.

Mum wasn't happy that I refused to accept I was bipolar. She didn't phone me again.

Through Glenn and my training at Unitec I was finding language for what was happening to me. Glenn showed me the cycles I was repeating, and gave me ways of breaking them. It wasn't easy.

I felt that life was unfair. I had been abused throughout my childhood and now I had to work at mending and healing my life, and to break the cycles. While I was consumed in therapy, wrestling my past, people I'd gone to school with were travelling, partying, building careers, getting degrees, having families and setting up homes. It was as though they had set sail on tall ships with the finest gear and sails, and were out on the ocean. Meanwhile I was still stuck at the dock with a broken and busted boat that I needed help to repair because I had no idea how to fix it myself. Instead of being able to get on with life I was having to address trauma. Yet I was determined to see it through.

¤ ¤ ¤

My girlfriend Sarah was the one who helped and encouraged me to get my driver's license. She knew more than me about cars because her family had taken the time to teach her.

Sarah was proud as punch when she got her first car. She and her parents checked the engine over again when they got it home. Her stepfather said that she needed to top it up with oil. Sarah handed me a 2-litre bottle of oil and asked me to do it, while she and her folks went inside.

Thinking that putting oil in an engine was just like putting water in a radiator, I emptied the whole bottle into Sarah's motor. Then I went inside and told Sarah she needed more oil because it wasn't full. Sarah just frowned and shrugged it off.

Later that afternoon Sarah and I went out. We had only gone a short distance down the road when the car started smoking and the engine began spitting oil. By the time we'd turned around and gone back home there was oil along both sides of the car, on the windshield and on the roof. It was everywhere. Sarah and her family were furious with me.

'You're a bloody idiot!' her stepfather snapped.

'Some mothers do 'ave 'em,' her mother remarked.

I went through a number of cars after I got my licence. Most of them weren't any good. I had a little Mitsubishi Mirage when I first started working at Mt Tabor. After six months of being there, though, I fell in love with a classic 69 Holden EK Special that was parked up outside the old Kaukapakapa Post Office. I had never fallen in love with a car before. The old Holden was in poor condition and needed work to be roadworthy but I approached the owner and he sold it to me for five hundred dollars. Heath, who worked and lived at Mt Tabor too, had worked as a mechanic and panel-beater in the past. He was a little older than me and was keen on helping me do the Holden up.

I decided to sell my Mitsubishi to raise funds for the Holden's restoration. So one Sunday morning Sarah followed me to the Ellerslie Car Fair in her car. I had kept my Mitsubishi in good condition and there was a lot of interest in it. A couple wanted it for their teenage daughter. We agreed on a price and the transaction was set to take place the following day, where we would meet and exchange the car for the cash.

Sarah and I headed back to Kaukapakapa. This time I was following behind Sarah. As I drove along I delved into my imaginary world. It was what I did whenever I was alone. My imaginary world had helped me to get through my childhood and teenage years. There was no better place to be growing up, and it was a place I still I valued and escaped to.

As I approached Albany and the end of the northern motorway, I was looking out my side window with my mind a million miles away. When I came to and looked back to the road ahead the traffic had stopped and Sarah's stationary car was coming up fast. I slammed on the brakes. My car arched and went under Sarah's car, slamming it forward. I watched Sarah's head bob up and down as her car slammed into a new Honda Prelude ahead of her. The occupants of the Prelude bobbed up and down as their car rear-ended a van in front of them.

'No, no,' I pleaded, hoping it was going to stop there.

The man in the van bobbed up and down as he was jolted forward. Thankfully the chain of collision didn't go any further. I had been in enough accidents by this stage to know that no one was hurt. I sat there for a moment in my wreck, considering the damage I had just caused. Dollar signs were raining down all around me. I had taken out three cars, plus my own car which I had just sold.

I got out and went to each vehicle and checked on the occupants. There was no whiplash, no scratches—everybody was fine. The man in the van calmly told me what I needed to do. I ran off to a pay phone to call the police. The old white man in the new Prelude from Orewa chased after me. He was yelling at people to stop me. He thought I was doing a runner to escape the scene.

I turned and told him off, calmly and clearly putting him straight, then made my phone call. The police instructed me on the procedure. There were no charges or conviction. Everyone was just happy that I'd taken full responsibility.

With no insurance I had to get money together to settle all of the accounts as a result of the accident. The couple still wanted to buy the Mitsubishi for their daughter, and were happy to wait for Heath to repair it. I had to sell the Holden to help pay for it all. Mt Tabor also helped with a loan so I could pay the rest of what I owed, and I was able to pay Mt Tabor back on a weekly basis.

'Wow, that was pretty spectacular, wasn't it?' Glenn, my psychotherapist, said when he found out about the accident.

We then explored who was behind the driving wheel of my life. It certainly wasn't a conscious adult. I was sabotaging my life and I wasn't even aware I was doing it.

Children from good homes attract good things. Children from homes like mine ... well, we attract the opposite. We are conditioned to seek the worst. We are most comfortable with what we know and are used to. We are programmed to self-destruct.

What I'd thought was my life wasn't my life at all. My every thought, action and decision was simply a consequence of the past.

When I was little my imaginary world had served me, but now I couldn't afford to leave my life under the direction of a wounded, unloved boy who felt worthless and unlovable. It was time to change—it was time for me to come out of my imaginary world and be present in the real world. In order for me to have the good life I craved I was going to have to root out the underlying beliefs and programmes in my mind that were setting me up to fail.

But was that even possible?

MT EDEN PRISON

Throughout my teen years I had been holding onto a possibility. It was more of a hope really. My biological father, Peter, was in prison. He had spent most of his life in prison.

I knew that he had raped women and children, but he was serving his time. Was it possible that he had changed? Couldn't he be a better man now? I wanted to believe so.

I fantasised about Peter being a reformed, new and improved man who had taken responsibility for his past. I fantasised that I could finally have a father-son relationship—a real one with a parent who wanted me and who loved me. A father who could rescue me from my life. I imagined the two of us spending time together, looking out for one another, and everything working out for the better. We would be a real family.

When I was eighteen I decided it was time for me to find out about Peter for myself, so I visited him in Mt Eden Prison. I had to see him outside of normal visiting hours because he was being kept separate from the main prison population due to the nature of his crimes. Child sex offenders are targeted in prison by the other inmates, who consider their crimes to be the worst of all.

I told myself that this was okay—his crimes were in the past. He'd no doubt changed.

I was led into the visitors' room and told to wait. A little later a few prisoners were brought in. A man who I guessed was Peter sat down in front of me.

He started telling me about some conversation he'd just had with another inmate on his block. I had no idea what he was talking about.

Then Peter looked at me. 'So who are you then?' he asked.

'I'm your son,' I said.

Peter jumped to his feet. 'Shaun!' he cried.

'No,' I said. 'I'm Tim.'

Peter's excitement dropped away. 'Oh,' he replied.

There was an awkward silence as he sat back down. I could see from his expression that I wasn't a good memory.

He looked me up and down with suspicion. 'What do you want?'

I started thinking that coming to see him had been a bad idea. 'I just wanted to meet you,' I said.

Peter was studying me, clearly trying to ascertain how much I knew. 'Fair enough,' he answered, relaxing a little.

We shook hands.

'I've been trying to contact Shaun,' Peter said. 'I've been leaving messages at his work.'

Shaun had told me that Peter had been trying to communicate with him. Loyal to Mum, Shaun had never replied to the requests. I had been wondering where my messages from Peter were.

Peter got me to tell him all about my life. I was open and honest.

Then he bragged about being good at fixing cars and gambling. He boasted about the amount of children that he'd brought into the world and of his prowess at judo. When he had finished bragging he talked about Mum.

'People think I have a temper.' He laughed. 'Boy that mother of yours. One morning I woke up in bed and she's sitting on me with a frying pan in her hands. She cracked me a good one with that pan. Another time I was working under the hood, fixing a car engine, and your mother slammed the bonnet down on me. She was a wild one that woman. She gave as good as she got.'

I had witnessed my mother's anger and violence first hand; I hadn't come here to hear about it from Peter. I wanted to know about him and why he was in prison. But rather than disclose anything real about himself, Peter wanted to hear about the abuse and violence I'd suffered. He blamed Dad for everything bad in my life simply because Dad was Māori.

It felt surreal to be sitting in front of a prisoner who'd been convicted of horrendous crimes, and have him try to tell me how bad my Māori dad was.

When I was growing up some of Mum's family tried to blame Dad for everything too. It seemed to be the default setting for the majority of my Pākehā relatives. Rather than look at their own abusive behaviour, it was easier for them to single out someone who was different.

I thought I should at least give Peter a chance so I remained in contact with him and members of his family, while maintaining a safe distance. Yet no matter how much I asked Peter he would never be straight up with me about his crimes.

Later he was released from prison. It wasn't for long though.

One day he phoned me. 'I need your help, son.'

'What's up?' I queried.

'Uh, I've stuffed up again.' He chuckled. 'I've hurt a little girl, and her family is out for my blood, so I need my sons to come around and protect me. Especially you, being a martial arts expert and all.'

I felt sick in my gut.

Peter was amused about the whole thing. He wasn't a changed man at all. He said the police were involved, but the family were wanting to take justice into their own hands.

I hung up, knowing that was the end of my relationship with my biological father.

All I could think about was the poor little girl he'd sexually assaulted.

I continued to have some contact with one of his sisters and her parents, but it wasn't much.

¤ ¤ ¤

In 2011 I visited a college up north and spoke to the students and staff about my life and how I had overcome my past and broken the cycle. As usual when speaking about my family I didn't say names and made sure not to give any identifying information away. However during my talk there was a stir at the back of the hall. A large family seated at the rear were looking at one another, nodding and talking while pointing at me. I realised they had recognised someone in my story.

Following my talk, students came up to speak to me and ask questions. I noticed that the family members were hanging around, waiting. I braced myself when the students moved on and the family came forward.

'We know who you are!' a woman fired at me.

'Do you?' I asked cautiously.

'Yep, and we know who your father is!' Her arms were crossed and there was anger in her face and voice. 'Your father is Peter,' she said. 'Your father hurt our family.'

'I'm not my father,' I declared, feeling my face starting to burn. 'I don't have anything to do with him.'

'He hurt a couple of our young ones,' the woman continued.

'I'm very sorry to hear that,' I replied.

'Can you help us?' she asked.

'If I can,' I answered.

'We want justice for our girls,' the woman explained. 'Peter sexually abused them. He tricked all of us. Would you be willing to talk to the police?'

'Yes, no problem.' I nodded. 'I will do whatever I can to help, but I didn't grow up with Peter—I only met him again as an adult—so I'm not sure if any information I have will be useful.'

'We need all the help we can get,' the woman said. 'He's a monster.'

'Yes,' I agreed. 'He's hurt a lot of people.'

A few months later I was asked to come into the Henderson Police Station where I was interviewed by a detective. The detective was heading up a team that was building a case against Peter involving historical acts of abduction, rape and molestation.

The detective hoped I might have some information on Peter that could help them. He explained to me that my father was a prolific sex offender. There were multiple cases connected to him, and the police believed that what he had been convicted of was only a fraction of what he'd actually done. The detective described Peter as a violent, predatory man who was incapable of behaving any other way.

'He's a monster,' the detective said. 'He's damaged so many lives, so many families.'

I recounted the little I knew about Peter, and about the last phone call I'd had with him many years ago, when he'd admitted that he'd hurt a little girl.

'Mum always told me that I was the outcome of rape from Peter,' I said to the detective.

'I believe her,' the detective was quick to reply. 'Peter would be one of the worst sex offenders we have on record.'

¤ ¤ ¤

One day at Mt Tabor there was a knock on the door. I opened it to find a Māori man standing on the front step. He was around the same age as me.

'Are you Tim Tipene?' he asked.

'Yeah,' I said.

'Kia ora, bro,' he smiled. 'I'm your brother.'

I had never met him before, but it turned out his name was Murray and he was one of Peter's other sons. Murray and I hit it off straight away and started catching up on a regular basis.

Every time Murray came to visit me he would be in trendy clothes and be driving the latest-model car. He told me he had a high-paying job in Auckland City working with cars. I was impressed and looked forward to Murray's visits to see what flash car he'd turn up in next. One New Year's Eve Murray loaned me his latest car for the night so I could take a girlfriend out on the town. It was a little sports car.

'This is my brother's car,' I boasted to the girlfriend, thinking I was pretty cool.

The girl liked the car so much she pushed me out of the driver's seat and got in behind the steering wheel. I had to hold on for dear life in the passenger seat as she sped around corners along the scenic drive in the Waitakere Ranges. I tensed up on each bend, wondering if this was the end. In my mind I could see us flying off the road and ending up mangled in metal. The girl seemed to have a death wish.

I was relieved to return the car free of damage to Murray the next morning.

I didn't see Murray again after that and he wasn't answering his phone. Months later I caught up with an aunty on that side of the family.

'Where's Murray?' I asked. 'I haven't seen him for ages.'

'Oh, haven't you heard, Timmy?' she said.

'Heard what?' I queried.

'Murray's in prison,' she stated, 'for stealing cars.'

So much for my brother's flash job in Auckland.

I recalled the scary drive through the Waitākere Ranges on New Year's Eve, and realised that the car my girlfriend and I were in had been stolen.

Since meeting Peter in Mt Eden Prison I had connected with his English family. While there was a reluctance to talk about Peter and his crimes, some were happy to criticise the wayward, Māori Murray and blame him for the family's issues. It was the same projection that members of Mum's family had put on Dad, and that my family had put on me. I knew I had another older Pākehā brother and a younger Māori sister from Peter that at the time I hadn't met, yet Murray was the only one I was being warned about.

Murray was eventually released from prison, but I haven't seen him again. At one stage, while high on P, he poured petrol over himself, lit it and tried to drive down the northern motorway. He didn't get very far. He ended up in hospital and then later was back in prison.

MONSTER

It was a moonlit night when I climbed out of the window onto the roof. The room I shared with Kenji was on the second floor of the house. Our window opened out onto the roof of the first floor, so it was an easy place to get to. It was an ideal spot to sit and look out over the valley at the rolling paddocks, the trees, and the Kaipara Harbour beyond.

But this night I wasn't looking at the valley. I was looking up at the full moon, crying and pleading to God. I was fifteen and frightened.

Throughout my childhood Mum had told me I would end up being just like my biological father, Peter. She said I would be a monster and that I would hurt women and children. That I would be a paedophile and a rapist.

Mum was a staunch believer of heaven and hell, good and evil, and after watching the film *The Omen* she started referring to me as the devil's child, with other family members following her lead. It's no wonder I identified with monsters in stories and on screen. The unlovable and the untouchable.

On a developing mind of a child, my mother's words had become a belief. From a young age I believed I was innately bad and destined to play out the same role as my father. I believed there was nothing that I could do to prevent it. I was cursed. After all, I was the outcome of rape.

Mum loved the Beatles. The day John Lennon got shot she was so upset she punished me. It was my fault. Mum always needed a focal point for her emotions, someone to blame. People were dying of starvation in Africa because of me.

I got to believing that I was a devil's child. I carried guilt and shame with me everywhere I went.

If someone fell over, I had somehow made it happen. Even if I was standing some distance away from them. If someone had a bad day it was my fault. I developed a habit of apologising for everything. I would even sometimes apologise ahead of time, just to cover anything that was about to happen. I apologised for my very existence. If I hadn't been in the world then surely these bad things wouldn't be happening?

¤ ¤ ¤

My family had been haunted by cycles of sexual abuse for generations. Both Mum and Dad had been abused, and the environment I grew up in was sexually charged. There were games of doctors and nurses that older cousins used to get me into their beds—and Licky Licky, where adults would chase us kids around, catching us and licking our bodies.

One incident of Licky Licky on me triggered both Mum and Dad. It was at a church picnic in a garden. My parents were always trying to fit in at such events, which was never easy for them when alcohol wasn't involved. I was ten and my family and I had only just arrived to the event when a woman targeted me.

'I like you,' she said, coming for me right in front of Mum and Dad. 'Licky, licky.'

I ran and the woman chased after me as though it was a game.

The church folk watched on, but they weren't laughing and nor were they trying to intervene.

I ran to the edges of the garden hoping to find a way out. I knew the woman wouldn't be able to catch me in an open space, however there was no gap in the hedges. She had me cornered. I was stuck and what was worse was that I had now separated myself from the others.

The woman tackled me to the ground, overpowering and smothering me with her larger body. I was helpless.

'Hmm, you're tasty,' she said, pressing her groin against me repeatedly and sticking her tongue out long to lick my neck and face.

I looked at the church goers. This sort of thing usually took place when no one else was around, surely they weren't going to let it play out right in front of them in broad daylight. Even I could see that this woman was not right in the head.

However everyone just carried on as if the abuse occurring before them was nothing more than innocent play.

Mum and Dad were watching. They didn't look happy.

Mum had told me that I wasn't to get my clothes dirty and here I was lying in the grass and dirt.

Dad got up and came over. He pulled me out from underneath the woman.

Unlike the catamaran at Mathesons Bay, Dad wasn't going to leave me to drown this time.

The woman just laughed it off.

Dad led me back to the picnic.

'Stay away from her!' he growled quietly, as though I was responsible for the woman's behaviour.

I appreciated Dad's intervention. He hadn't done that before, and he didn't do it again.

As a small child at parties I would be put to sleep in some room where adults were openly having sex on the same bed as me.

All the time I was growing up my body had never been my own. Adults and teens had used me as a child. They would make me touch them. They would fondle and grope me, penetrate. Mum said it was my fault, that I was a dirty little bastard.

Most of the kids I hung out with—cousins and friends—had been sexually interfered with. It was a secret we all shared. Whenever I met new kids it wouldn't take me long to work out if we shared the same secret. A lack of boundaries, isolation and a need to connect were the main signs. Abuse was what we had in common and we found comfort in being close to each other. It was what we had been taught.

I was only little when we lived in Massey, west Auckland, with Peter, but I remember the fear in that house. As a youngster my mind was plagued with images of sexual violence. I knew of things that other kids didn't. I would dream of women and children being grabbed, dragged to a concealed spot and forced down. In my innocence and confusion as a child I would play these fantasies out in games with other kids. It all reinforced Mum's message that I was a monster.

There were few boundaries in my family and us kids took our lead from the adults around us. Once at the hot pools I was part of a group of people that went down the hydro slide together. We were an entanglement of bodies spiralling up, down and around the tube until we burst out into the pool of water at the bottom, where a crowd of spectators were lined up at the fence watching.

When I emerged from beneath the water I found an angry Māori girl who looked to be around the age of ten standing directly in front of me.

She slapped my face. 'Don't touch me, ya pervert!' she yelled.

People cheered.

My face burned red with embarrassment. I was twelve and had no idea what was going on.

I found out later that a much older white cousin had been groping the girl while coming down the slide. She had assumed it was me since I was near her at the time. My cousin boasted about it and laughed.

This wasn't the only incident where my older white cousins set me up. Another time a group of us had piled into my older cousin Greg's car. He was at the wheel and his girlfriend, Nancy, was in the front passenger seat. The rest of us were crammed in the back with little room to move. At twelve I was the youngest in the car. I knew Nancy and her family from church, and was friends with her brother. It was late and dark, and during the ride back to the house a male cousin in the back snuck a hand around Nancy's seat and grabbed her breast. Nancy was quick to cry out and complain.

The cousin responsible said I had done it and pointed out that I was the one sitting directly behind Nancy. Once again I had no idea what was going on. With all the bodies in the car I was pinned against the back seat and could barely move, let alone reach Nancy. I told Nancy I would never do that to her.

The touching in the dark continued though, and the situation escalated with Greg threatening to punch me out for touching his girlfriend. When he pulled the car over to the side of the road to confront me I got out and walked.

That same year a man had gotten me alone in the public toilets at Matheson Bay. The beach was almost deserted that day and I had gone into the toilets to get away from the strong wind and rain. The man followed me in.

Guarded, I kept my distance, but seeing that I was alone the man took an interest in me. He asked about my life and why I was on my own. We chatted for a bit. I thought he was just being friendly. I was desperate for adult attention and here was someone who seemed to want to spend some time with me.

The man stepped closer. Standing over me, he took my hand and used it to rub his erection up and down. I did as I always did when being sexually abused. I froze. In my mind I started to run through the repertoire of what sexual acts he might want me to do.

But unlike all my previous assailants he gave me an opening. Rather than just taking, as the others had done, he tried to convince me into letting him do more. He wanted my consent.

'No, I have to go,' I said, trying to pull my hand back.

He held my hand firmer, pressing it against himself. He said that he wanted to fuck me. 'It'll feel good,' he said.

'No.' I shook my head.

I pulled my hand back again, finally getting free, and edged towards the door, saying sorry and that I really had to go. The man tried to follow, but once I was out the door I ran.

In this instance I managed to get away, but I believed I was responsible for such encounters. That they were purely my fault and that I was attracting this response from people by giving out the wrong message.

So now, at the age of 15, I sat on the roof looking to the sky and begging God for help.

I didn't want my mother to be right about me. I didn't want to be a monster. I was petrified of becoming a paedophile and a rapist.

I didn't know how to be close to someone without it being sexual. Even as an adult my mind would instinctively go into trying to work out what sexual act another adult wanted from me whenever they spoke to me. I was conditioned to perform and please, and to know that adults wanted only one thing from me. That I was good for only one thing.

I had tried to get control of my sexualised behaviour before, yet it hadn't worked. But that night, there on that roof, at the age of 15, I made a deal with myself and God. The deal was that I could have sexual contact with any consenting adult, but nothing outside of that. It didn't bother me that I might be further abused; I just wanted to ensure I wasn't the one doing the abusing.

At the same time I made the decision not to use alcohol or drugs. I hated the smell of alcohol. I remembered the fumes from men on top of me, pinning me down from behind, smothering and hurting me. I also figured that no matter how uncool I might appear to other teens for not drinking, I needed to stay in control if I wanted to stay safe.

It was a crucial moment in my life. I made a rule for myself, and it was a rule that I would never go back on.

I didn't become a paedophile. I didn't rape or molest anyone. I've never abused or hurt another person.

Unfortunately what I did do was cement a desperate, compulsive, promiscuous behaviour that led to me having many sexual partners throughout my life, and in all these relationships I re-enacted my childhood sexual abuse and as a result victimised myself even more.

I might not be Peter, but instead I ended up following in my mother's footsteps. Mum was promiscuous. She liked getting attention from men. She would call out to them on the street, push her trolley into them at the supermarket. Now and then Mum would have to drive her and us kids all over the countryside because some man she'd flirted with was following her home.

My promiscuous behaviour left a path of failed relationships and drama, which only added to the guilt and shame I already carried. Yet for me it was a far better choice than the alternative.

I admire and appreciate that desperate, isolated 15-year-old that I was. He was my champion. That time in the moonlight stands out clearly as a life-changing moment for me. While I continued to carry the guilt and shame of being a monster well into my forties, I never played out the role.

KATIE

One night when I was eighteen a girlfriend drove me home. When we walked into the house we could hear a noise coming from Katie's room. I opened the bedroom door to find my 15 year-old sister in bed with some man in his thirties. The room reeked of alcohol.

Having been interrupted, Katie told me to get out. I went and sat with Sarah in my room and discussed what I should do about the man in my sister's bed. Mum was in Gisborne with her new family, Shaun was in a small town down south and Dad was with his girlfriend in Kaukapakapa. Katie had been living at the homestead on her own until I had been allowed to move back in. I had no authority in the home or over my sister. I was powerless. Sometime during our conversation the man left.

A few days later a friend of my sister's pulled up in a car with some mates at the end of our driveway. The girl tooted the horn and called out, so Katie went down the drive to meet her.

But it was a setup. As soon as Katie stepped out of the gate, a much older, larger woman and her sister got out of the car and beat Katie up. By the time I realised what was happening, got downstairs and raced outside the woman and her mates were driving away.

I asked Katie if she was all right, but she wouldn't talk to me. With tears in her eyes she marched into the house and into her room.

Later that afternoon Dad turned up. He too shouted for Katie. When she went out to see him, he slapped her across the face. The slap was so hard I heard it from inside. When I went outside Dad was back in his car and driving away. Katie was holding the side of her face.

'Did he hit you?' I asked.

Katie nodded.

I wanted to go after Dad. It was one thing to hit me, but to hit my sister? That made me angry.

It turned out that the man in Katie's bed had preyed on her. He had gotten her drunk to get her into bed. Everyone in the community had found out about it, and the woman who'd attacked Katie outside the gate with her sister was his partner. Dad was embarrassed. But instead of confronting the man who'd had sex with his underage daughter, Dad chose to hit Katie. It was a classic case of blaming the victim.

Katie believed she'd got what she deserved. She saw herself as the bad, rebellious kid, and it was convenient for the family, school and community to reinforce and perpetuate that belief. It hurt to see my little sister treated this way.

Mum and Dad both failed Katie. They had even allowed my older cousin, Greg, to get into her bed.

Greg was in his twenties when he started having a sexual relationship with 13-year-old Katie. Mum, Dad and Greg's father, Uncle Todd, knew about it, as did other white relatives. While the parents weren't happy when they first found out, they still allowed it to continue. Mum adored her handsome nephew—Greg could do no wrong—so he would come to the family home and spend the night in Katie's bed.

I never liked it. Katie was my little sister. Yet again I was powerless to do anything about it.

Years later Katie told me that Greg, his brother Daniel and their Pākehā mates had all been pushing their way into her bed. Sometimes they would fight over her, and it wasn't just Katie. It was her friends too. The boys would buy the young girls cigarettes and alcohol. Katie said it had been happening even before she turned 13. It's no wonder then that some days Katie was turning up to school drunk.

As I am writing this my daughter is around the same age now as Katie was then. In sharp contrast to Katie's childhood, I have always taken responsibility for my daughter's welfare and security. To this day I have ensured that she is safe and free to grow up without being abused or interfered with, just as her older brother is.

FACING DAD

It was the weekend of Katie's 13th birthday. Her white, skateboarding boyfriend, Carson, had stayed over the Friday night before the party. He was to sleep in the room Kenji and I shared.

Mum and Dad turned up late that night. They arrived separately and both were drunk. Mum had come from town and Dad from the local. It wasn't long before they were arguing with one another. After a while Dad yelled out for me. I left Carson sitting on Kenji's bed, reading his skateboard magazine, and went downstairs.

I walked into the master bedroom. Dad had Mum up against the wall. It looked playful at first.

'I'm going to hit your mother, boy,' Dad threatened.

Dad never hit Mum. He wouldn't dare—he was too scared of losing her. The only people Mum allowed Dad to hit was me and Kenji, and Dad followed Mum's rules. I should have remembered that, because of course it's why he'd called me.

I went straight into standing up to Dad in order to protect Mum. I couldn't see that I was playing right into my parent's drama.

Dad slammed me against the wall. 'Do you remember, boy?' he growled. 'Do you remember what I did to you when you were little?'

His fists were clenched tight, gripping my top. He pulled me forward and slammed me against the wall again and again. 'Do you remember!' he kept yelling.

'That's enough!' Mum shouted at Dad, trying to get in between him and me. She kept grabbing at Dad's face to get eye contact. 'Don't,' she said.

Mum wasn't wanting to remember.

She distracted Dad, allowing me to head back upstairs to my room. But Dad followed after me. The two of us ended up standing directly in front of Carson. Dad grabbed me by the collar and punched me.

Carson didn't move. The poor boy stayed seated on the bed, his attention fixed firmly on his skateboarding magazine as though nothing was happening.

'Do you remember!' Dad yelled.

'Let him go!' Mum cried, suddenly appearing through the doorway and cracking Dad on the back of the head with the broom.

Dad clutched his head with his hand and dropped onto one knee. Mum ran down the stairs.

Carson's eyes never lifted from the magazine. Kenji was nowhere in sight. He had already bailed, having climbed out the window onto the roof when he heard the arguing escalating downstairs.

Although Dad was kneeling, holding the back of his head with one hand, he was still gripping my shirt with his other hand. I reached under my pillow and pulled out my Nunchakus and raised the weapon. I was determined Dad wouldn't hit me ever again.

Mum suddenly reappeared. 'Don't you hit your father!' she cried.

'He hits me,' I argued.

Mum told me to get downstairs.

I wrestled myself free from Dad's grasp and got out of the room. Carson was left sitting on the bed, his gaze having never shifted from his skateboarding magazine. Dad was still on one knee in front of him, clutching the back of his head. They were now the only two in the room. In his drunken and confused haze Dad must have thought it was me sitting there, since he had never met Carson.

'It's all your fucken fault!' he growled, grabbing him by the collar.

Carson spluttered and gasped as Mum and Katie rushed into the room.

'Leave my boyfriend alone!' Katie cried.

They wrestled Carson free from Dad and got him downstairs. Carson and I escaped outside and hid in the back of Mum's car, locking ourselves in I was pleased to have a comrade in action. I don't think Carson saw it that way though.

I could see Kenji hiding in the shadows up on the roof.

Dad came outside to see why Mum, Katie and Shaun were standing around Mum's car. They'd basically given me up. Dad saw me hiding in the back and started trying to smash the car window to get at me. Shaun was now bigger and bulkier than Dad. He got in his way and held him back.

Using the distraction, I got Carson and me out the door on the other side of the car and we ran, jumping a fence and sprinting off into the dark. Carson followed me across a large paddock and into the bush. There we hid among the trees, shivering in the cold and watching to see if Dad had followed. Dad wasn't good out in the natural elements, so I was pretty certain he wouldn't find us.

Sometime later Katie came over to the bush and called out to us. She told us it was safe to come back. I didn't trust her judgement, so Carson and I stayed put. Finally, in the early hours of the morning, we crept back to the house. Mum got us to hide upstairs in the loft above the garage. I thought that it was a stupid idea—the pull-down ladder was the only way in or out of the loft, so Dad would have us trapped. But I did as I was told. Carson and I shared a single mattress for the rest of the night. We didn't sleep much.

¤ ¤ ¤

Now and then Katie would take off. To begin with she would hitch around with her mates. Then Mum and Dad bought her a car, a Ford Escort. They said it was for her and me, though I wasn't allowed anywhere near it. Katie wasn't supposed to drive it until she was old enough and had her licence, but she wasn't going to let that stop her; and it wasn't long before there were no adults living at home to stop her anyway.

One time when she disappeared my girlfriend Sarah and I spent hours unsuccessfully searching for her. Eventually Sarah drove me back home, and we walked into my room to find a mess. I realised Dad must have come home, realised Katie was missing, and been so furious he'd gone into my bedroom and smashed my stuff. I didn't own much, but the majority of what I did own had been shattered.

'But you didn't do anything wrong,' Sarah argued as she helped me clean up.

She left, and later Dad returned. I went downstairs to meet him. He came in through the door all tough and yelling at me, but stumbled back when he found me directly in his path. He tried to have a go, yet something was different. Dad was keeping his distance. I could see he was scared. He knew he'd gone too far this time.

I went back to my room and sat with the broken pieces of my life. I could hear Dad moving around downstairs. I figured he was staying for the night.

I reflected on the fact that life wasn't working out for me. I had been kicked out of school and I had no job prospects, and now the little I had owned had been smashed. But I remembered I still had weapons. Dad hadn't found those. I had kept my martial arts weapons hidden away so they couldn't be stolen. I got out one of my hunting knives. I decided that this was it. I'd had enough. When Dad went to sleep I was going to kill him. Dad would never touch me or damage my life again.

I sat on my bed and waited. Later I heard Dad go into his room. I ran the knife through my hands. In my mind I kept going over how I was going to end him. I didn't care about the law and being arrested, I just knew there was no going back.

A couple of hours passed. I looked out the window to see the shine of the master bedroom's light reflected on the darkened lawn. Dad would normally be asleep by now. Something was up. He made a lot of noise downstairs, broadcasting the fact that he was awake.

He knew.

I could feel it. Dad knew that I was coming for him. He was staying awake on purpose.

I continued to wait. As time ticked on my thinking began to change. If I went through with killing Dad then nothing would get any better. It would only get worse. I still had hope that one day I would get away from the abuse and violence, and get away from feeling powerless. I wanted to make a better future for me. I wanted to make something of myself and live a happy life.

I didn't have to be like Dad. I could be a better person—better than him and Mum. I could rise above their choices and behaviours.

As I twirled the blade about in my fingers I wondered why I should belittle myself through a violent act and ruin my life because of Mum and Dad. If I had any chance at a good future then it wasn't going to be in killing. I had to get away from them. Get out from under their darkening madness. That was the only way forward.

Calmer, I put the knife under my pillow and got beneath the blankets. I now knew that Dad was scared of me. He wouldn't be coming upstairs.

While no one had been killed, there had been a death this night. It was the death of the petrified, powerless little boy. I wasn't little now. I was no longer petrified and powerless. Dad couldn't beat me anymore. Things were changing.

¤ ¤ ¤

A few years later I faced Dad again. Mum had left her bank job and set up a café in Palmerston North. I went down for the opening. Dad was there too, as well as Mum's new partner, George. Dad was staying out of the way. He sat at a table outside on the deck. Throughout the evening Mum kept coming over, sitting next to Dad then going back to George.

'Bloody hell,' Dad said at one point.

'You all right?' I asked.

'I don't know what's going on,' he grumbled. 'Your mother keeps touching me under the table.'

I could see that Dad was getting upset. He kept watching Mum with George.

By the end of the night Dad was drunk and angry. Everybody else left, but Dad was determined he wasn't going anywhere. Shaun tried to get him out and couldn't, so he asked me for help. I knew this was the chance I'd been waiting for.

At the time I was still living in fear—sleeping with a light on every night and keeping a weapon close to the bed. Even though I was now an adult, a martial arts instructor with black belts who was trained in security and close protection, whenever I closed my eyes to sleep I reverted back to being a traumatised, powerless little boy. I was plagued with nightmares of abuse and violence, and because of this I rarely slept. Hypervigilant, I was constantly on alert, and it was exhausting. It didn't matter if it was day or night, I was primed, pumped and ready for action.

I was hoping that if I changed the dynamics further with Dad then it might settle my fear and anxiety.

Shaun and I approached Dad. He was sitting, leaning over a table, swaying with his head down, eyes fixed on the floor.

'C'mon, Dad,' Shaun said. 'Time to go.'

Dad laughed and shrugged him off.

'Let's go, Dad,' I said, calmly.

Dad went quiet.

This is it, I thought.

Sure enough, without lifting his gaze Dad started swearing and threatening me.

I bent over and looked him straight in the eye. 'Pardon?' I said in a low, firm voice.

'Uh, nothing, nothing,' Dad slurred, raising his hands in surrender. 'Sorry, boy.'

He got to his feet and came along with us quietly.

Through being calm and direct I had let Dad know that he would never lay another hand on me. I was confident I could look after myself without hurting him. It was over.

Dad never threatened me again.

In projecting his pain and rage onto me, Dad had passed on a shadow, just as it had been passed on to him. Yet I chose not to hurt him or anybody else. Instead, I was choosing to dissect and pull the shadow apart, making sure the cycle of abuse and violence would end with me.

Dad wasn't happy about it though. It bothered him that I hadn't hit back because he knew it had showed up his own behaviour.

'You just think you're better than us!' he would spout.

WANTING TO BE DIFFERENT

It was a Friday evening, the end of a working week, and on a country road I stood between a car and a van. The vehicles were facing one another with their headlights on. In the van were my workmates from Mt Tabor. They were pleading with me to go out with them.

'C'mon on, Tim,' Martha said from behind the wheel. 'Come to the pub. It won't be the same without you.'

'Yeah,' Darren, another mate, echoed from further in the van. 'Let's have a good night out.'

I looked at the car where my girlfriend, Jo, sat in the driver's seat with her two young nieces sitting in the back. It was dusk, and in the fading light I could see them watching me.

'You need a night out, Tim,' Martha said.

'Yeah, but...'

I didn't know what to say. I didn't want to disappoint my mates and I liked being included. After months of psychotherapy I was now venturing out more into the world with a confidence I'd never had before. I had started going to the pub with workmates and had even started drinking. Previously I had felt awkward at social events and avoided them. I didn't know how to be around others.

'Okay, okay,' I said to the van. 'I'll be straight back.'

I ran over to the car and opened the driver's door.

'Hey, dear,' I said. 'I'm going to go out with my mates tonight.'

I could see the disappointment in her eyes.

'You promised, Tim,' she sighed. 'You said we were going to have a night together. I got us movies to watch, and snacks.'

I cringed. The last thing I wanted to do was to let Jo down. I was desperate in all of my relationships—desperate to be loved.

I had been going back and forth between the car and the van a few times now, trying to appease the occupants of both vehicles. I didn't want to upset either party, but each time I said 'no' their attempts to persuade me had increased. All eyes were on me. I was starting to feel hot and flustered.

'Please, Tim,' Jo said.

'It's just tonight,' I explained to her. 'We can do something tomorrow.'

She looked away, studying the lights of the van ahead.

I tutted and stepped back, then took hold of the driver's door with one hand and pushed it shut. However the door didn't just shut—it slammed and the window shattered, spraying glass over Jo and the two small girls in the back. I hadn't even been aware that I was feeling so angry. I had only meant to close the car door.

There was silence, a deafening silence, as the occupants of both car and van looked at me. They were all waiting to see what I was going to do next. I eyed my hands.

This wasn't the man I wanted to be. I remembered looking at Mum and Dad when I was a small child and saying to myself that I was never going to be like them when I grew up. And now, here I was. It was a still night, yet I raged inside. Had I become my parents? Had I become a monster?

I eyed the two little girls and Jo. They looked frightened.

'Is anybody hurt,' I asked, scanning them for any sign of injury.

It took Jo a moment to reply. She had been expecting my anger to escalate.

'Is anyone hurt?' I asked again.

Thankfully no one was physically harmed—there were no cuts or bleeding—but they were shaken and scared.

'I'm so sorry,' I stuttered. 'I'm so sorry.'

'I know,' Jo replied.

'Just wait here,' I said.

I could feel the shame burning across my face as I came up to the van. Its passengers were now subdued. I wanted to crawl into a hole and hide.

'I'm sorry everyone,' I said sheepishly.

'You all right, Tim?' Martha asked.

'Yeah,' I nodded, showing everyone in the van that I was now back in control. 'I'm staying here.' I explained, looking back at the car. 'I've got to sort this out.'

'Okay, Tim,' Martha replied. 'You take it easy, eh?'

After I had cleaned up Jo's car, she and I ended up having a nice, quiet night at home with her nieces, watching videos and eating junk food. Yet I couldn't let the night's events go. My anger had gotten the better of me, and I didn't like that. It was as though I was walking around with a loaded gun that was ready to go off.

It was one thing to want to be different from my past, but another thing entirely to *be* different. To be different meant work was required. The psychotherapy with Glenn, personal development training at Unitec and martial arts I'd done weren't enough. If I wanted a good life, free from my past, I was going to have to do more.

'I can't drink,' I told myself. 'If I want to be different from my parents—if I want to be in control—I can't afford to drink. I have to remain conscious and in control.'

I returned to the pledge I'd made when I was fifteen and turned my back on alcohol. I didn't like the taste anyway, and the smell of it always brought back memories of abuse and violence.

¤ ¤ ¤

One evening a few months later I walked into a building in Auckland. I had enrolled in a course on anger management and living without violence.

When I entered the room I found a large half-circle of over twenty men. They were all seated and facing the front. None of the men seemed happy. It was obvious they didn't want to be there. Since there was only one chair left on the end of the half-circle I sat there. I appeared to be one of the youngest men present.

Two affluent-looking white men walked from the back of the room up to the front and sat on chairs facing the rest of us. They were the facilitators for the course. The pair seemed different from everybody else—as if they had come from privilege.

One of the facilitators stood and greeted everyone. Then, starting from the opposite end of the half circle from where I was sitting, he asked each man his name and what had brought him to anger management. The second facilitator remained in his seat, verifying and ticking each name on a clipboard. It was all very serious and official.

As each man spoke it became apparent to me that they had all been sent to do this course. It was conditional of criminal convictions and court orders. Many of the men had been sent for beating up their partners, while others had been sent for assaults outside the home.

Surely not everyone's been forced to come? I thought, looking at the men ahead of me. I was hoping I wasn't the only one who had chosen to be here.

The facilitator continued around the half-circle, drawing closer to me.

I cringed. *I'm not going to look very cool,* I thought.

As the last man before me spoke I realised no other man had come of his own free will. I was the only one who hadn't been sent by an authority.

The facilitator looked at me. 'What brought you here?' he asked.

I could feel my face turning red as I mumbled my answer.

The facilitator got me to repeat it louder because he hadn't heard me the first time.

'I just want to sort out my anger,' I said.

'And who sent you?' the facilitator asked.

I cleared my throat. 'No one.'

I had everyone's attention. The facilitators didn't believe me.

'Someone must have sent you,' the one standing remarked.

'What is your name?' the other asked.

'Tim Tipene,' I said.

He got me to spell it out as he ran through the list on his clipboard. 'He's not on the list,' he remarked to his colleague.

'How did you find out about this course?' the first facilitator queried.

'I just phoned up and said I wanted to do anger management,' I answered. 'I was told to come along tonight.'

One of the men near me frowned. 'What, so you volunteered to be here?'

'Yeah,' I nodded.

'Why the fuck would you choose to come here?' another man asked. 'Haven't you got anything better to do? Go home, man.'

'Yeah, go and watch the rugby, bro,' another added.

'I'd rather come to anger management of my own accord than have someone in authority send me because I've hurt someone,' I said.

There was also the fact that I didn't trust anyone in authority. The police had already shown that they had little interest in my welfare—they had already tried to lock me up rather than address the violence in my home. There was no way I would ever give the authorities power over me and allow them to dictate my life.

I was out to prove everyone wrong about me. I was a good man and I would show them all. I would not let the past damage my future. I remained in the course, and at the end I was asked to come on board as a trainee facilitator. I jumped at the opportunity, because what better way to learn about anger and how to manage it than to be a facilitator of anger management and living without violence courses?

So as a young man in my early twenties I ended up working with men old enough to be my father—and they were all my father. They were hurt, damaged and angry just like him, and I had to help them find a way through it, and help them find freedom in taking responsibility for their actions.

The very freedom that I was finding in taking responsibility for my life.

TIPENE

It was a lady from Telecom who taught me how to pronounce the name Tipene correctly.

It had been just me and Katie at home when the phone rang and I answered it. On the other end was a Māori lady from Telecom. She asked to speak to Mr or Mrs Tipene, but she said our name wrong.

'That's not how you say our name,' I said. 'It's Tippanee.'

The phone went quiet.

'Excuse me?' the lady said.

'Our name is pronounced Tippanee,' I repeated.

'Oh no, no, no, boy,' the lady muttered. 'Your name is pronounced Tipene.'

'Eh?' I frowned.

'That is how you pronounce your name,' the woman continued. 'Tipene.'

I looked around. I thought the lady was pretty cheeky telling me that I, at fifteen years of age, didn't know how to say my own name. Tippanee was how Dad and everybody else had always pronounced it.

'Now you say it back to me,' the woman said.

'Pardon?'

'You say the name back to me,' she said. 'Tipene.'

I was smiling and frowning at the same time. Was Telecom now in the business of teaching people how to pronounce their own names? Was it some new service they were giving to customers?

'Come on,' the woman urged.

'Tipene,' I said.

'That's it,' she replied. 'Now say it again.'

'Tipene.'

The lady made me repeat it seven more times. 'Now you make sure you pronounce your name correctly,' she said. 'You are very lucky to have a name like that. You should be proud of it.'

The woman said goodbye and I hung up the phone, then stood for a moment, thinking how strange the call had been.

'Hey, Katie?' I called.

My sister came out of her room.

'We've been saying our name wrong,' I said. 'It's not Tippanee, it's Tipene.'

Katie frowned.

'A lady from Telecom just told me,' I explained, pointing at the phone.

When Dad came home Katie told him. 'Hey, Dad,' she said, 'we've been saying our name wrong. It's Tipene.'

Dad just shrugged it off. He didn't know.

None of my family line were speakers of te reo Māori. I became the first to learn the language, and because of that I became the speaker for my family by default. I tried to get out of speaking, but that wasn't possible for a Tipene who would become the creator of Warrior Kids and an award-winning author.

In the late 1990s I was invited to speak about Warrior Kids up at a marae in Kaitāia. I took an uncle and aunty with me to speak on my behalf during the pōwhiri. My uncle did a great job, and my aunty followed up with a beautiful waiata.

When they sat down, though, the wharenui was still. I kept my head bowed, eyeing the floor in front of me. People coughed. The uncomfortable silence grew.

Just wait it out, I told myself. *They'll move on.*

But they weren't moving on.

My uncle looked at me.

Then a kuia from the marae stood.

Finally, I thought.

However the old woman crossed the floor, took me by the hand and led me to the taumata, where she left me standing on my own. I had no choice but to speak.

From that point on I was expected to speak at every event I attended. I have done many te reo courses now, yet I am still struggling and have a long way to go before I will ever feel confident to speak.

THE WOODEN BIRD

Mum admired Uncle Todd, especially his wealth. By the time I was ten she had moved on from working in a burger bar, had gotten herself a job in a bank and was well on her way to climbing the corporate ladder. She was very excited the day she got to fire her first person after being made supervisor. I couldn't understand what there was to be happy about, considering someone had just lost their job.

Uncle Todd liked to travel overseas and holiday in other countries. He encouraged my parents to come along on one of his trips. We went to Fiji. Mum and Dad loved it so much we went twice.

On the first trip we stayed on Malolo Lailai Island. I spent the duration of the holiday away from my family and the Plantation Island Resort, where were staying. Instead I hung out with two local boys, Sava and his brother Miitii, who were around the same age as me. Sava and Miitii invited me into their home up in the hills, and introduced me to their family and to the large framed picture of Jesus hanging up on their wall. The boys showed me the Island way of life.

On the second visit to Fiji a couple of years later I was 12, and spent even less time with my family. We stayed at Castaway Resort on Qalito Island this time. Peter and Abraham were two young Fijian men who worked there. They liked talking with me and got me to tag along with them and other staff while they worked.

In the mornings Peter and Abraham took me out on a boat to feed the tiger sharks food scraps from the resort. Peter would then dangle a small line over the side and catch remora, also known as suckerfish. The remora stick to the underbelly of the sharks, where they remove parasites.

Back on the beach, Peter and Abraham made a fire and placed the gutted remora on top. After a little while the men pulled back the burnt skin of the fish, revealing the cooked flesh. Peter and Abraham brought out some homemade brew which tasted just like pineapple juice. Here I was, a twelve-year-old white boy, on a beach in the Pacific, eating fresh fish and drinking with Fijian men. I was in paradise.

One evening Peter and Abraham took me behind the resort to the workers' quarters. While the rest of my family were in the bar enjoying the entertainment put on for the tourists, I was in a flat out the back with a large number of the resort staff, drinking homemade brew. In the early hours of the morning Peter and Abraham snuck me through the resort back to the chalet where I was staying. I was drunk for the first time in my life. Peter and Abraham had laughed and enjoyed my singing with them earlier in the flat, but now they just wanted me to stop singing because they were worried someone would find out. I was certain Sakapo wouldn't have approved, and this mattered to me because as well as being an elder on the island, he'd taken me under his wing.

I first met Sakapo on the large boat that had taken me and my family from the main island of Viti Levu to Qalito Island. I noticed the old Fijian man looking dignified and chiefly as he sat up tall on the top deck of the boat. I'd noticed him because he was staring at me.

When I went near him he spoke to me. He was a quiet, reserved man, his presence calming and steady. In Māori terms he had a lot of mana.

Like Peter and Abraham, Sakapo took a special interest in me. Perhaps it was because I seemed to be on my own, separate from my relatives. On the island he showed me his carvings and gave me lessons on how to carve. He carved a wooden bird for me. We would sit beneath the coconut palms and talk for ages. Sakapo tried to teach me how to climb one of the palms. He also taught me how to play pool. I spent hours hanging out with him every day.

'You are like a son to me,' he said.

I felt it too. Sakapo was my father for the entire time I was on the island. He seemed to need me as much as I needed him.

Shaun took a photo of Sakapo and me standing on the beach. My family's holiday was ending and we were waiting for a boat to take us back to the mainland. Sakapo and I were standing off to the side away from everybody else. My head is down and my hands are in my pockets. Sakapo is looking out to sea. We are quiet.

The photo is a reflection of how we were both feeling. I knew Sakapo didn't want me to go, and I didn't want to leave my new-found father. I had experienced more love from this man in a few days than I had in my entire life with Mum or Dad. It was as though I'd been back with the whānau.

It seemed so wrong. Here were two people wanting to be together—a man wanting a son, and a boy wanting a father—yet I was leaving with parents who didn't want me at all.

Tim and Sakapo

When I hugged Sakapo for the last time I didn't want to let go.

On board the boat I was thinking of how I could sneak off and get back to him. For the remainder of the trip I kept touching and smelling the bird Sakapo had carved for me.

¤ ¤ ¤

Years later, when I was 18, my girlfriend Sarah and I spent a night under the stars on a bank overlooking the Kaipara Harbour. I had set a net to catch mullet and flounder. I was out to impress her with my fishing skills.

It was a romantic evening during which Sarah told me a story. When she had finished she asked me to tell her one. I had been working on a story, but I still didn't have it all figured out. I was going to have to ad lib.

My story was about a boy who lived on an island in the Pacific. The boy wanted to help his mother and father, but he was too little. Then one day the fishermen of the village returned with no fish and the villagers had to go hungry. As each day passed there was still no food for the village and the people became angry. So the boy set out to make his father happy with the help of his uncle, who was a carver. I had been developing the story ever since my time with Sakapo in Fiji, and I called it *The Wooden Fish*.

My girlfriend was impressed. 'That was amazing,' she said. 'You should write it down.'

'Nah,' I said.

But I did. I wrote it down and put it away for safe-keeping.

A few years later again I read the story to another girlfriend.

'Wow, that's a great story,' Michelle said. 'Who wrote it?'

'I did,' I replied.

It took some convincing for her to believe me.

'You should do something with that story, Tim,' she said. 'Don't sit on it.'

'What do you mean?' I frowned.

'You should look at getting it published,' Michelle suggested. 'Do you know anyone who could help?'

By chance I had met a lady called Jill Eggleton when I was sixteen. My girlfriend at that time, Eloise, was mates with Jill's daughter and we had spent a Sunday afternoon at their flash house with a pool. Jill had taken some interest in me while I was there so I felt I could approach her. I knew she had been a schoolteacher and that she had had books published.

I managed to get Jill's phone number through Eloise. I phoned Jill and asked her if I could send her a story to see what she thought. She was happy to take a read.

At the time computers were becoming a thing, so people were throwing out their old typewriters. I had found one such typewriter on the side of the road in an inorganic collection.

I sat at the typewriter and typed up my story. I had done typing at school for a term and could recall where I was supposed to place my fingers to access each key. It was going to take me a while to get into a rhythm with that though, so I resorted to just using two fingers.

Once I had finished I posted my story off to Jill.

A week later she phoned me. She loved the story. 'You've got gold here, Tim.'

She explained that she was sending the story back, and warned me that she had made some corrections and not to be alarmed when I saw it. Jill then encouraged me to type the story up again, making her corrections, and send it off to a publisher.

'Don't even stop to think about it, Tim,' she said knowingly. 'Just fix the story up and send it off.'

When I got the manuscript back there was red pen all over it from where Jill had made corrections. *The Wooden Fish* had gone from being a short novel to picture-book size, but as I read through the edited version I knew it was now perfect.

With my two fingers I typed the story up again. I then wrote up a nice cover letter to go with it, just as Jill had advised. I went to the local bookshop and looked in the front of the New Zealand picture books to find the names and addresses of publishers. With that information I sent my story off.

A few months later and my relationship with Michelle was over. I ended up flatting in a house in Helensville. I was alone for my birthday and didn't hear from anyone. That wasn't unusual though—I had long been in the habit of celebrating Christmas and birthdays alone. At Christmas I would put up a tree, and on my birthday I'd buy myself a cake and a gift. I would even put candles on the cake and sing happy birthday to myself. Just because no one else was going to celebrate my birthday didn't mean it wasn't going to be celebrated. Sometimes, though, I would feel sorry for myself and end up crying over my cake. This's how it was this year. However some amazing gifts in the form of letters changed that.

First I received a letter from Learning Media, who wanted to publish my story in the *School Journal* with a collection of other people's stories. I was so excited I didn't hesitate. I phoned them up straight away and said yes to the publication. Learning Media posted out the contract and I signed it without a second thought.

Then three more letters arrived, all from leading publishers wanting to publish *The Wooden Fish*. However these three all wanted to produce it as its own book and not in a journal. Oops, I had rushed in.

I was ecstatic though. It was my first story that I had ever sent to a publisher and I had four wanting to buy it. My primary school teacher, Miss Foote, had told me I was a writer, and she was right.

I had been kicked out of school and deemed a failure. I had just been dumped by my girlfriend for not being enough—though guess who wanted me back as soon as she heard the news?

The Wooden Fish was published in 1996 in *School Journal* Part 2, Number 3. It was the opening story. Reed Publishing offered to publish the story as a stand-alone book when the two-year contract with Learning Media expired. In 1999 they did just that, hiring Jennifer Cooper to illustrate it, and it later became a Storylines Notable Book.

Following the publication of *The Wooden Fish* I took on the idea that I was an author. That all I had to do was touch the page and it would turn to gold. I got out my old typewriter, wrote loads and loads of stories, sent them all off to the publishers, and sat back, awaiting my fame and fortune. Every one of those stories was sent back, rejected.

Yet I had done it once, so I knew I could do it again.

Five years after *The Wooden Fish* was first published, my second book—*Taming the Taniwha*—was published and became an award-winner.

I have a lot to be thankful for. If my girlfriends hadn't encouraged me with my first story I don't know when or even if I would have gotten around to sending a story to a publisher. Also, I'd had a lot of rejection by this stage of my life, and whenever I was rejected I turned around and went the opposite direction, so if that first story had been rejected I might not have ever tried again.

I had written *The Wooden Fish* as a tribute to Sakapo—a man I had only known for about ten days and who had inspired the story. However guilt got the better of me, and in feeling disloyal to Dad I had a dedication to him put in the front of the book. After all, the story is about a boy's gift to his father.

Dad couldn't have cared less. Perhaps on some level he felt that he didn't deserve it, but it seemed to mean nothing to him.

AFFLUENTLY HIGH

My old schoolmate Michael and I climbed into his Mk 5 Cortina with tinted windows and headed for the Coromandel Peninsula. I had talked him into attending a native American sweat lodge retreat with me. Since Michael is part native Canadian he was interested in connecting and understanding his culture more.

We weren't happy about the price of the course. It was expensive and we were both struggling financially, yet we had committed to giving it a go.

During my last year at high school Michael had been involved in an accident. He and another mate had been riding on their motorbikes and had collided front on around a bend in the road. Michael came off worse. He had deep burns and gashes in both legs, and in one leg there was only 30% of the kneecap left. It took Michael a while to recover and a lot of painkillers.

Then a year later Michael reacted to a new type of drug he was taking to treat his type 1 diabetes. He had a seizure in the shower and collapsed, knocking the hot tap on full. He lay conscious, but unable to move, as he was burnt from the head down. It took Michael's family some time to realise what was happening and bust open the bathroom door that Michael had locked. It was his second time in the rescue helicopter.

I had to be careful when I visited Michael in hospital and make sure I wasn't sick and that everything I wore was clean, since there was concern about Michael catching an infection. Michael was covered in burns and had lost one of his ear lobes. His new party trick was that he could blow smoke out the hole that was his ear.

Due to both accidents and the numerous corrective surgeries that followed, Michael was basically living on painkillers for a few years. It was a hard time for him. He had always been a handsome, outgoing young man, and there were plenty of girls who had liked him. Now he wasn't feeling so confident. He referred to his body as being like Freddy Kruger from the *Nightmare on Elm Street* movies.

The plan was for Michael to get a synthetic ear lobe attached, but in the meantime he was given a temporary one that stuck to the side of his head with Velcro. Michael didn't like it because the Velcro was faulty and the earlobe kept falling off.

Michael would sometimes attend my Ninjutsu classes. One night I got him to help me demonstrate some evasive moves to a group of adult students. The students all lined up to watch. I stood in front of Michael with a wooden sword raised above my head. I stepped forward and struck out, swinging the sword diagonally downwards at Michael. He responded perfectly by leaping back to evade. However when he did so his ear lobe dropped to the floor right in front of the students. The students' jaws dropped at the sight of the ear on the ground.

Michael instinctively clutched the side of his head with his hand. 'Uh, shit, my ear.'

The students were horrified, thinking I had just cut off Michael's ear.

Seeing the student's reactions I couldn't help but laugh, which made the students think I was a complete madman. As Michael stepped forward and picked up his ear the students looked at one another and started to back away. I was laughing so hard I couldn't reassure them.

Now Michael and I were off to a native American retreat together. It was an opportunity to get away and do something spiritual. When we drove up the long drive with our windows down and AC/DC booming loud like the bogans we were, we couldn't see any sign of indigenous Americans. What we did see was affluent, middle-aged white men standing around outside. They watched us as we roared up.

Michael and I looked at one another.

'What the fuck is this?' Michael queried. 'Is this the right place?'

'Yeah,' I said. 'Maybe there are more people inside.'

We decided to give the retreat the benefit of the doubt.

The organisers got us to sign in. It was then that they informed us that we would be fasting for the first day.

Michael and I looked at one another again. This course was costing us both a fortune and now we were being told there would be no food on the first day?

Michael explained that he couldn't do that. He was type 1 diabetes — he had to have food.

The organisers weren't convinced. They maintained there wouldn't be any available.

Michael and I were both wondering if this was really the right place for us, especially with the middle-aged white men taking native American names and dancing around as though they were members of a tribe.

There was also no way Michael was going to fast—it would be too dangerous for him. I suggested we head off up the road and get some food, but Michael had another idea. That night in our room he produced a container of muffins. These were Michael's special muffins, made with cannabis.

'I'm going to have these,' he said.

Michael knew I didn't drink or do drugs, and that I didn't mind if he did. But on this occasion he wanted me to have a muffin with him. 'Just one,' he said. He'd always wanted to see me high. He thought it would be funny.

'No,' I said, sticking to my commitment.

'C'mon, just this once,' Michael said. 'We're in a safe place and I'll look after you. No one will know. Don't let me do it on my own.'

I was feeling bad for having dragged Michael down all this way for a phoney native American experience. The cost of petrol to get here was enough on its own, let alone the retreat fees.

'Okay,' I said. 'Just this once.'

I took one of the muffins. Michael was a good cook and the muffin was delicious.

When we'd finished eating, we chatted and waited for something to happen. I had no idea what to expect since I'd never been high before.

After a while Michael looked at me. 'I thought the muffins would be strong,' he said, 'but there's nothing. Let's have another one.'

We were both hungry after fasting, so another muffin went down the hatch, then another. We continued to talk and eat till late into the night, and eventually fell asleep. In the morning I woke feeling my usual self, and wondered if I had experienced a high or not.

'We must have slept it off,' Michael said.

We were already late for the morning session so we got ourselves together and went down to the main hall to join the other men. When we walked in we were both gobsmacked. All of the men were out on the front lawn, naked in the sunlight, doing what appeared to be a sun dance.

'Shit,' I said, looking at Michael.

The men carried on with their dance as though we weren't there. Michael figured we should join them. He started stripping off and I followed.

I couldn't believe it—all that money for a course, and on the first day no food and now no clothes.

Michael walked right through the group of men, found a place to stand on the side and started to join in the sun dance. I wasn't walking that far. I just grabbed a space in the middle.

I was trying not to laugh at the naked men surrounding me, but was finding it increasingly difficult not to. Something was happening to me. Perhaps it was the combination of sun, fresh air and lack of food. Whatever it was, it was clear to me that the muffins from the night before had been triggered and I was starting to lose it.

I looked about for Michael, knowing that I needed his guidance because I could feel my control slipping away. 'Michael!' I whispered loudly. 'Michael!'

But Michael was in no better state than me. While all the men continued with the sun dance Michael was off in another world, doing his own dance to the universe.

I was on my own. I tried to retain control and go along with the rest of the men, but it was no good. I collapsed into a heap on the ground, pointed at each man and his penis, and laughed out loud hysterically. I couldn't stop laughing. Even after the sun dance had ended and the men had left the lawn I was still on the ground, laughing, and Michael was still doing his own dance.

Following our performance we were asked to leave. We thought it was a good idea too.

We chucked our things into the Mk 5 Cortina, wound down the tinted windows and waved goodbye to the men, then turned AC/DC up and drove away.

I returned to my commitment not to do drugs, and never ate Michael's muffins again.

MOKO MĀ

I had remembered that twenty firsts were significant in the whānau and were always celebrated with a big party. I recalled the food, the music, the dancing, the laughter, the connectedness of everyone, the gift of a key—and of course the alcohol and the fights. But that was a long time ago, and while Mum and Dad had celebrated Shaun's twenty-first with a party, it was Mt Tabor that put on a party for me. It wouldn't have happened otherwise.

I invited Mum and Dad, and I appreciated that they came. Dad even brought a keg. We didn't talk much though. Roger and the other people of Mt Tabor were more of a family to me.

Katie and Shaun were there, as well as some friends, including my childhood mate, Vincent, whom I hadn't seen since primary school. He got to meet my puppy, which I had named after him.

The big surprise for me though was when Nana Tipene and Aunty Nan walked in. Nana knew that it was my 21st. All these years I had thought that she had forgotten about me, but here she was. Somehow she had gotten the details of the party from someone. I don't know how she did it. It was awkward for me because I hadn't seen her and Aunty Nan for so long, but the fact that she was there meant everything. It felt like I was waking up from my first eye operation all over again. I wasn't alone. I had been told to stay away from the whānau, but I was my own man now. From that point on I started visiting Nana and my uncles.

Having had so much time apart I wasn't sure how to be around the whānau, or even if I had a place with them, yet they kept opening their doors to me.

Nana uplifted my grandfather from Waikumete Cemetery and took him home to Rīpia on the Kaipara, near Dargaville. After that she sold the house on Swanson Road and moved up to Dargaville too. Katie and I would drive up there to see her.

Then Nana got sick with cancer. Now when I visited I would sit at her bedside and rub her head.

It was the 8th of August, 1997 and I was at Haranui Marae on a te reo Māori course when I got the call from Aunty Mabel to tell me that Nana had passed. It didn't take me long to get back to Rīpia Marae, a place I vaguely remembered from my childhood.

I helped carry Nana's coffin onto the marae.

'Who's that Pākehā?' a young woman spat when I walked into the wharenui.

'Shut up!' Aunty Yvonne Kingi-Waru growled. 'That's your cousin!'

Dad turned up to the tangi late, and by then the kaumātua had already been talking about him in their speeches, pointing out that Nana's eldest son wasn't there. When Dad walked in he was drunk, and just sat there as the speech-makers berated him.

I felt for him.

Later that night there was a big bang outside. We all came out of the wharenui to find Dad's van in the ditch. He had tried to get away unnoticed, but in his drunken state he'd driven off the driveway and straight into a ditch. He was stuck there now.

The ground in our urupā is sandstone and notoriously hard, so Uncle Blake and Uncle Robert Waru got a jackhammer to dig up the top layer of my grandfather's grave, so that Nana could be laid above him. However since the All Blacks were playing Australia my uncles decided to go to the pub and watch the game, putting off the digging till the next day.

Early Sunday morning Shaun and I followed our two uncles out of the marae and across the road to the urupā. It was a peaceful and tranquil morning among the graves.

My brother and I could only look at one another as our uncles started up the jackhammer.

'This doesn't seem right,' Shaun said.

I agreed.

Sure enough Uncle Rob Sarich, our kaumātua, was quick to march across the road from the marae.

'What are you doing!' he yelled.

The uncles carried on jackhammering, pretending not to see him.

'Oi!' Uncle Rob cried, making them turn off the machine.

'It's Sunday morning,' he said. 'The Lord's Day. This is not the right time. You should have done this yesterday.'

The grave got dug later and I'm pretty sure Uncle Mike Waru took lead in that.

On the last day of the tangi, when the lid was placed over Nana, I wailed. Rīpia is one of my home marae, yet I felt disconnected. A stranger. Nana was my last link to the whānau and to a time when I'd felt loved and treasured. That was all gone now. I felt as though I no longer had a place.

I still had my uncles with special needs, but I didn't have Dad or Uncle Blake. They weren't interested in the whānau. They were saying they couldn't wait to see the back of Rīpia, and that they were never going to return, vowing to be buried any place but there.

Following Nana Tipene's tangi I made efforts to stay connected with the whānau. I felt that I owed it to my grandparents, Aunty Joy and the rest of my elders for all that they'd given to me. After all, I carried their name.

I was grateful to my Aunty Nan and Aunty Mabel who kept me in the loop of what was happening, and I attended marae committee meetings with Aunty Mabel. There were more tangi, including that of my Uncle Robert, aka the mayor of Te Atatū, and my Uncle Lyle, Dad's other brother who had only just returned from living in Australia.

I was unconfident with my identity, yet being at the marae was second nature to me. I set tables, cooked, cleaned dishes, cleaned toilets, spoke during pōwhiri, and dug graves. It had all been installed in me as a child, and was what had made me so good at my job at Mt Tabor.

My grandfather had been the chairperson for the whānau committee and my Aunty Sammy Larkins and Aunty Nan encouraged me to follow in his footsteps. I didn't last long in the position though—not after some whānau started complaining about a Pākehā being made chairperson. My aunties were disappointed when I resigned. I stayed away for a while, yet the Māori world always had a way of pulling me back.

After one tangi my girlfriend Catherine and I started on our journey back to Auckland. It was at a time when the people who remembered me as their white moko were becoming fewer and fewer, and I was wondering if I really belonged. Not far out of Dargaville my car broke down.

A farmer came out and tried to help. He got me to sit behind the wheel as he fiddled with the engine. 'Try it now, Tim,' he'd say periodically.

I would turn the key and try to bring life back to my car.

'That'll do, Tim, that'll do,' the farmer said each time as though I were one of his farm dogs.

Catherine and I couldn't stop laughing.

The farmer managed to get the car running again, but it only got us a short distance.

'Seems that someone doesn't want you to leave,' Catherine remarked.

I had been thinking the same thing.

In the end we managed to get the car to a repair shop in Wellsford, and got picked up from there. The next day I phoned the repair shop.

'There's no problem with your car,' the man said. 'We've checked everything and it's running fine.'

From that point onwards I never had another incident with the car. So it seemed very strange.

A couple of years later I was on an authors' tour up north. I was feeling weird, passing through areas that were connected to my whānau and not visiting anybody.

One evening I spoke to an audience in Karekare. I had my books to show, as usual, and midway into the talk I picked up *Taming the Taniwha*. It fell open to a photograph of my grandfather.

There are no photos in *Taming the Taniwha*. Somehow the photo had ended up in between the pages. The sight of it caused me to jolt, which in turn startled the audience.

I apologised, told them what just happened and showed them the photo. Everyone laughed. I placed my grandfather's photo down and carried on with my talk. When I turned to the next page of *Taming the Taniwha*, there was a photo of my grandmother.

'They're both here,' I said, showing the second photo.

Much of the audience were amused by my shocked reaction.

'They've come with you, Tim,' one woman said.

The influence of my grandparents, my aunties and my uncles had always been present throughout my life. It wasn't just in my name. It was in me—in my dreams, in my writing and in everything that I did.

Even the matriarch of our whānau, Aunty Nan, acknowledged it in the wharenui at Naumai Marae.

'You might be white, My Timmy Me, but everything you do is Māori,' she said. 'Your books, your talks, your work with children and families. They have all come from your Māori side.'

It was what had been ingrained in me, and was what I knew.

In 2016 I returned to the position of Chairperson of the Nga Uri o Hetaraka Waitai-Tipene Whānau Committee. There were no objections this time. Not only did I have Aunty Nan's backing, but also the support of Aunty Martha—our matriarch from the Hetaraka line.

The first nine months proved to be a tough for the whānau with eight tangihanga in that short time. Two to suicide.

Whenever I tried to make a date for a committee meeting someone would die or be in the process of dying. We'd barely get over one before there was another. I spent much of the year keeping everyone up to date with the condition of loved ones, hospital visiting hours, and the locations, dates and times of tangihanga and funerals. I was also doing a lot more whaikōrero, and although I have done a number of courses in te reo Māori I have proven to be a slow learner and still have some way to go.

My life had come complete circle. I was back with my whānau. When Nana died I saw Dad as my only link and he wanted nothing to do with the whānau, but I've come to understand that I am my own link. I carry my grandfather's name; I am his namesake. I am the white moko of my matua tupuna, and I have represented them and my whānau in all that I do. I know that Dad and Uncle Blake have their reasons for staying away, but their experience is different from my experience. In 2020 I was appointed Secretary of the Rīpia Marae Whānau Committee.

KURA TOA

Having gotten away from my immediate family—away from the violence and abuse—my life had changed. My day-to-day existence had become more settled and calmer, and things were going well for me.

However the effects of my childhood abuse and trauma were still present. Night time was when my hypervigilance was at its worse. I kept a light on through the night and a weapon next to my bed. The slightest noise or even silence would have me up, stalking through the house with a sword raised and ready.

Girlfriends had come into my room at night, only to have me jump out of bed at them with a pair of nunchakus.

'It's me, Tim!' they would cry. 'It's me!'

Aside from psychotherapy, my martial arts was the biggest help to me in overcoming my past. After becoming independent I had been able to return to Sensei Peter Lee and Go Shintai Kai Karate. I was attending multiple classes and trained hard, getting myself up to optimum fitness. When I was asked to help teach the art I jumped at the chance, knowing that I was a step closer to my dream of being a professional martial arts instructor.

Normally I wasn't confident around other people, but when it came to martial arts I just came alive and took charge. I knew what I was doing and felt exhilarated after teaching a class.

Having the freedom to attend karate also meant I could return to ninjutsu, so I enrolled in Sensei Michael Gent's Togakure-Ryū ninjustu classes in Whangaparaoa. Wanting to learn as much as I could, I also explored other martial arts.

Once I started going up the grades I left Mt Tabor to follow my teenage dream of being a full-time teacher. It was just after my 21st.

Mt Tabor had been good to me and it was hard to leave, however it was certainly the right time. After living there for over two years and going through psychotherapy with Glenn, the professional development training at Unitec and having the love and support of the Mt Tabor community I was feeling ready to face the world. I wanted to test my new found skills and confidence. I would miss the people and was certain that they would miss me. Especially Roger. However I stayed involved over the years. At one point I was a Mt Tabor trustee, then an advocate for Roger and other members of Mt Tabor, sometimes I worked shifts and one year Roger even came and lived with me and Catherine.

After leaving Mt Tabor I found a place to rent in Helensville that would take me and my dog, took a course in Close Protection (Bodyguarding), and started doing part time security work. I also joined the army, becoming a weekend soldier in the territorial forces.

I achieved a 2nd dan black belt in Go Shintai Kai karate and judo, and the title of Chief Instructor. In ninjutsu I gained my 1st dan black belt and taught classes under Sensei Gent.

During the day I trained and in the evening ran classes. I taught karate, judo, ninjutsu and women's self-defence. I believed that if I put the hard work and effort in, it would pay off in the long run. I still had to rely on other work though, since there wasn't enough income to survive on.

I had classes in Helensville, Kaukapakapa, Orewa and Dairy Flat. I discovered that my mum's father had taught wrestling in Helensville. It was amazing to think that I was following in my grandfather's footsteps.

Sensei Michael Gent ran his martial arts school differently from Sensei Lee. As a teen, Michael shot a man. This led to him going through a number of correction facilities wherein he connected with gangs and became a member. On the street Michael was known as The Assassin, and he'd been in an estimated 300 fights. He said that if he ever wrote his life story he would be arrested.

Rather than continue down a path of crime, Sensei Gent chose to put his energy into the martial arts. His school was a gang that wasn't a gang. Our patches were written in Japanese kanji. Sensei Gent offered a place for misfits, a family. The bulk of his students had come from the hard side of life. We trained hard and realistically. There was blood and broken bones in classes. Ambulances were called. I had new cuts and bruises every week.

For me Sensei Gent became a father figure. I was spending nearly every day at his house. I would mow his lawns, run his errands, drive his girlfriend around. I even helped him clean out his father's house in Dargaville. I went all over the country with Sensei Gent. He trained me, and he trained me hard.

For my 2nd dan black belt grading for Go Shintai Kai karate I had to spar against another instructor. We were around the same age and I saw it as an opportunity to test my skill.

The man faced me in his stance.

I glared at him as though he were already dead, just as I had been taught to do. His legs started shaking first, then his hands and arms. He trembled all over. Before the fight could even commence he started to cry.

'I'm not doing this!' he yelled, and left the floor.

I had defeated him without even touching him, intimidating him to the point of shattering his spirit. Those in the fighting community would probably be proud. I wasn't.

The man got changed out of his uniform, walked out and never came back to Go Shintai Kai. He had started karate as a boy, and over many years had worked his way up the ranks. He was a soft man, a caring man. He was a good teacher for children, and for him it was all over.

I may have got my 2nd dan, but it was nothing to be proud of. I had destroyed a man from the inside. This wasn't the person I wanted to be.

¤ ¤ ¤

One Sunday afternoon three of my adult students and I went to a field to train. I had the men grab a weapon each and got them to attack me. Going up against multiple opponents was what I liked best. The more challenging the better.

The men went for me and I dealt with each of them. In the end the men were all on the ground, hurt and beaten.

'Get up!' I roared. 'C'mon, don't stop! Let's go again!'

The men didn't move.

'C'mon!' I cried.

'No way,' one of the men said, shaking his head. 'You've lost it. This isn't training. You're just beating us up.'

In that moment, in my mind, I left the field and journeyed back in time. I was no longer a man, but a little boy, and Dad was standing over me. Dad was so much bigger compared to my little frame. About three times the size. It dawned on me that I was recreating the past. I was the little boy going up against Dad in the form of three grown men. I had done this training over and over again, but no matter how many men I hurt and defeated I had never won. Because each night I was still being woken by nightmares of a little boy being hurt and abused by his dad.

I was being governed by my past, with fear and hurt still dictating. This had nothing to do with my students. I was abusing them.

I apologised, but the introspection didn't stop there. I was continuing to work security as a bouncer for bars and clubs, and as a doorman for upmarket restaurants. I was also security for politicians during an electoral event and even a bodyguard for Mickey Mouse, Minnie Mouse, Donald Duck and Goofy when Disney brought them to New Zealand for a tour. Believe me, Mickey and his crew had serious security. We even had ear pieces at one point with 'The mouse is on the move' coming over the com.

It was because Ronald McDonald had been beaten up a month before in Australia by a group of youths. From that point on entertainers for children required security.

My highlight in security work though was in 1995 when I was a security courier for CHOGM, the Commonwealth Heads of Government Meeting, which was held in Auckland.

My role was to deliver gifts from the NZ Government to the hotel suites of all the world leaders. There was the Sultan of Brunei and even the Queen, but the one who stood out for me was Nelson Mandela.

I was hoping that I might actually get to see him when I went to his room, but I didn't. A few days later, though, I got to see him when he spoke at an event in the Auckland Domain. It wasn't close and personal as it would have been if I had gotten to meet him in the hotel, yet I'll never forget it. Mohandas K Gandhi, Martin Luther King and Mandela were all inspirations for me and the list has only grown.

¤ ¤ ¤

One of my security roles was at a female strip parlour in town. There had been an incident where one bouncer had thrown a patron through the shop window of a neighbouring business, while another bouncer had stomped on a patron who was lying unconscious on the pavement. The neighbouring businesses had complained and I had been brought in to bring a more professional approach. The other bouncers didn't like me being there because they knew they were under scrutiny from management. I didn't like being there either—I thought it was the worst place for me considering my ongoing wrestling with compulsive, promiscuous behaviour.

One issue the parlour was struggling to deal with was the boyfriends and husbands of the girls performing. The girls' partners would come in and sit among the patrons to watch. Over the course of the evening the partners would become upset with seeing their girlfriend or wife performing for men. Some of the girls would even provoke and incite their partners, knowing that the bouncers would intervene. We kept an eye out for jilted partners who might threaten or try to physically abuse the girls, and we watched for weapons.

One night a man attempted to enter the parlour. As he came in through the door I noticed he was concealing something in his jacket with his right hand. I clamped the man's hand in place so he couldn't pull whatever it was out and guided him back outside. It turned out that he was only concealing a bottle of beer that he'd brought from another bar. However he was clearly too intoxicated to be allowed in the parlour. I remained outside, preventing him from entering.

Angry, the man stood up in my face and threatened to take me out. He spat at me and described all the ways he was going to hurt me. He was Māori and looked a lot like Dad, even being around the same age. He wanted to fight me, but I just stood there keeping my composure and holding his gaze.

The man's verbal attack lost all power when he started to insult my mother. I had to keep from smiling at that point. I was tempted to say, 'Oh, so you know my mum?'

Soon the man stepped alongside me. He stayed there for a while, watching the world go by.

Finally he tutted. 'I'm sorry, man,' he said.

I looked at him and saw tears in his eyes.

'My wife's left me,' he said. 'She took the kids.'

In the early hours of that cold morning we ended up having a counselling session right there on the sidewalk. The man cried. He wasn't happy with where his life was. It was much later, when the effects of the alcohol were wearing off, that he left. He gave me a hug before he went.

I thought how things could have been very different for this man if it had been one of the other bouncers.

A lot of training and focus in the martial arts is reactionary. It is based on a belief that the world is a threat, that people are out to get you, and that one must always be prepared. Like an action movie where there is good and bad, and in order to win one must defeat the other. There was little willingness to consider different perspectives or to understand complexities. This training only increased my hypervigilance.

I wanted to be part of the solution, not the part of the problem. This man on the street reminded me of Dad and Mum. I love my parents, and they were once children. As monstrous as their behaviour has been towards me, they were still people. There is a story to the choices they had made in their lives, just as there was for Peter's behaviour. For me it's not about excusing the behaviour. It's about understanding it so I can change not only my life, but also the lives of others. This influence was coming through in my classes.

One afternoon I was walking down the main street of Helensville. A woman from my self-defence course fell on her knees in front of me. She was crying and saying thank you over and over, and causing a scene. People were looking at her and at me. I could feel my face burning. I wanted to run away and hide. It turned out that during the self-defence course the woman had been living in an abusive relationship. The course had empowered her and been a catalyst for her to leave her partner. I was starting to see that I was in a postion of influence, that what I was doing was having a positive impact.

I was moving away from teaching under the banner of Go Shintai Kai Karate and Togakure-Ryū Ninjutsu, since my classes had morphed into something entirely different. They had become a mix of martial arts, therapy and personal development, all steeped in Māoritanga. What I called Toatoi.

I was drawing on my childhood through concepts such as Manaakitanga and Whakawhanaungatanga, offering to others what my whānau had taught and given to me.

Since leaving Mt Tabor I had gone through a number of relationships, and lived and worked in various places, but nothing had worked out long term. I had tried enrolling to become a schoolteacher, but was rejected. The only thing that was working for me were my classes.

So in 1994 I made the change official by starting my own school. I called it Kura Toa Warrior School. Steering away from the traditional martial arts model of standing in fixed lines, I brought in play, adding warm-up games and making the classes more of an adventure. The kids especially liked the sharing circle where they each got to talk about a high point and a low point from their week. My classes began to grow, proving popular with kids and their parents. The parents appreciated the self-control and social skills aspects of the classes.

The adult students weren't so keen on the direction I was heading in. As far as they were concerned they had sought out Master Tim Tipene, the Chief instructor of Go Shintai Kai karate and instructor of ninjutsu. They wanted to learn techniques for hurting people, not talk about their feelings.

But I had moved on. As far as I was concerned, strong on the inside meant strong on the outside. When it came to physical techniques my focus had changed too. Influenced by my experiences in security and in working with adults who had special needs, I was now teaching techniques of de-escalation and containment, seeking to solve conflict in non-violent ways.

In making the changes to what I was teaching I was able to continue to work on myself personally. I believed that the direction I had taken would ultimately help me break the cycle of abuse and violence I'd been raised in. It would help me be a safe person, and it would keep me aiming towards a better future.

On a deeper level my classes were justifying my existence. I was the outcome of rape. I still carried the belief that I was evil. I didn't feel worthy of life. I was out to prove to everyone that I was essentially a good man, deserving of love and acceptance.

My creation was also an act of rebellion. It was an 'up yours' to the school that had kicked me out and to the teachers who had looked down on me. It was a middle finger to the community that had condemned and villainised me through gossip and projections, to the police who had tried to lock me up, and to a world that simply didn't care. I was showing them all up; I was showing them that they were wrong about me, that I was really a decent man who did good things.

I also formed the classes out of frustration. There had been no classes or programmes to help kids like me when I was young—kids from troubled homes that everyone was waiting on to mess up and go to prison. My class for children was the class I had needed and wanted when I was growing up.

¤ ¤ ¤

I called my children's class, Warrior Kids. I charged a gold coin per class, though a number of families got to do the classes for free. I wasn't making any money, but I was turning my pain into purpose, and that meant more to me. Through my classes I was out to save the world, and also the little boy within.

Parents were finding my classes a great support. They would stay and watch, and comment on how they were learning too. Through teaching I was able to model constructive methods of addressing behaviour. Parents felt safe with me. They trusted me and knew I wasn't out to judge and condemn.

One mother approached me after a class. 'I need help please,' she said. 'My boys just won't listen. I don't know what to do. I'm hitting them—I'm hitting them with sticks—but they still won't listen.'

I was able to guide the mother away from physical discipline to safer and more effective ways of being with her sons.

There were times of crisis within families and I was there to support them. Families were splitting apart, struggling to deal with tragedies or stumbling their way through generational cycles of violence and abuse. Police and government agencies were often involved. There were moments where I felt overwhelmed.

Complete strangers would turn up to observe the classes. I didn't mind. I liked to keep an open-door policy. Some were parents looking for ideas, others were teachers and health professionals. There were some who even sat there and took notes. It only bothered me when people poached my ideas for the development of their own programmes and classes.

All of the programmes for adults that I knew of in the community were reliant on funding. When the funding dried up those programmes ceased to exist. I wasn't going to let that happen to Warrior Kids, so I ran it without funding.

With ongoing classes children didn't have to stop after ten weeks—they could keep attending. This allowed families to come for as long as they wanted and to move on when they felt ready.

The students were also able to earn belt grades, just as they would in any martial art. However the grades reflected the individual's own growth and achievements, which meant that children earned grades for different things. One child earned a grade by preparing and cooking his parents a three-course meal. The photos of that went far and wide. A teenage boy was awarded a grade when he prevented a student from stabbing another at his school, thereby saving both students. Another child earned a grade for going up a reading level after struggling all year with her reading.

Each grade was personal and meaningful to the student.

THE SWORDSMAN

I had started Kura Toa and was now teaching Toatoi and Warrior Kids. However, to keep my own learning and skills up I would attend seminars from visiting masters.

I took part in a seminar with Dr Masaaki Hatsumi, the grandmaster of Bujinkan Taijutsu, formerly known as Togakure-Ryū Ninjutsu. I also attended a seminar of Shinkendo—traditional Japanese sword work—with Master Obata Toshishiro. Obata Sensei has been rated as one of the top Japanese swordsmen in the world, and is also an actor who has appeared in a number of Hollywood movies.

Throughout the Shinkendo seminar, for whatever reason, Obata Sensei picked on me. I became his crash-test dummy, used to display techniques to the other students. I felt extremely privileged, and while I couldn't see what was going on as he threw me around and tied me up, I certainly felt it.

'He likes you, doesn't he?' one of the other students said, laughing as I got up from the floor and stretched out the pain.

At one point Obata Sensei had me face down on the mat. He sat on my back and shuffled forward, taking my arms up my back towards my head. When I cried out in pain he slapped me hard over the head.

'You should be more flexible,' Obata Sensei said.

He then rubbed my head lovingly like a parent would a child.

Just as I was thinking that this was nice, Obata Sensei shuffled forward some more, pushing my arms further up my back and bringing me another bout of pain.

'Argghh!' I cried.

Whack! Obata Sensei struck me across the head again.

I was starting to wonder what seminar I had paid for.

The master rubbed my head soothingly, before shuffling further forward.

This went on for some time, much to the amusement of the other students.

On the last day of the seminar Obata Sensei presented me with his personal business card and invited me to be one of his students in Hollywood. I was so honoured. When I got in my car I just sat there, staring at Obata Sensei's card. He had been so fatherly towards me. I thought it would be an amazing opportunity to be one of his personal students, living in Hollywood. But it just seemed so impossible. At the time I had no money, no job and no home. I considered myself a failure.

So I shrugged the invitation off, thinking it was just an unrealistic dream I couldn't afford to dwell on.

Yet Obata Sensei hadn't given his card out to others. He gave it to me. He saw something in me that I clearly wasn't seeing myself. I had a chance at something more but I simply couldn't comprehend it. If I could go back in time and talk to the young man I was I would tell him to grab that opportunity—to get over to Hollywood and make the most of it.

I have kept Obata Sensei's card. His invitation was an affirmation in itself, and it propelled me onwards with my own classes.

¤ ¤ ¤

In 2009 I sat on my knees on the floor of a dojo in Japan facing a large audience.

Noguchi Shihan, a high-ranking Japanese instructor of Bujinkan Taijutsu, stood behind me with a wooden sword raised and ready to cut down at my head as Grandmaster Dr Masaaki Hatsumi watched on.

The spectators were on the edge of their seats, keen to see if I was going to get hit.

I closed my eyes, taking myself away from the crowd.

It was an achievement in itself that I had managed to get to Japan, let alone that I was now being tested for my 5th Dan black belt.

I relaxed, allowing myself to be fully present. Without a sound the instructor struck. Sensing danger, I bowed and rolled forward, evading the strike.

Dr Hatsumi and the audience clapped.

It was a pass.

Many fail the test and those who do are given the opportunity to try again, and again.

I only needed one attempt, and I don't say that to boast.

After the grading I was congratulated by high-ranking students, and my past teachers were praised for having taught me so well. But my survival instincts had been honed long before I ever stepped foot in any dojo. It wasn't any martial arts teachers who had sharpened my senses—it was Mum and Dad, and my abusive and violent upbringing, and I had come all this way to prove it.

I was confident with the grading because I'd been hypervigilant all my life. My senses worked overtime. As a child I had been able to sense the mood of my parents before I even opened the front door to enter the house after a day at school. I knew when it was time to hide and be quiet. The problem I had was how to turn the fight-and-flight response off.

A result of my childhood was that I became very good at martial arts. I could sneak around the house undetected, I could find my way in the dark, I could read situations, predict attacks and reactions, I could evade a threat and get myself out of danger. I knew how to take a beating and I knew how to fight and use anything as a weapon. I knew how to survive. My parents taught me. They were my first martial art instructors.

A few days before the grading I arrived at the hombu dojo early for my first class in Japan. I was out to make a good impression. I got dressed into my Gi and reached into my bag for my black belt, only to find that it wasn't there. My heart dropped. I pulled everything out, but I had obviously left my belt behind at the hotel. My uniform was incomplete. I had come all the way around the world to take part in these classes and I wasn't ready.

The school was well known for the large number of foreign students it attracted and catered for. I figured that visiting students must have left their belts behind before. Surely this school that serviced the international community would have a contingency plan for this sort of thing? Perhaps they had a belt that I could buy.

I approached an English-speaking senior Japanese instructor; he just shrugged. I spoke to two western instructors. No advice or help was offered.

Cultural protocol is important in Japan. I couldn't just turn up to my first class with an incomplete uniform. I felt that would be disrespectful to the Grandmaster. I figured it was better to walk out of the school and come back another day. The instructors and other students watched me get undressed and return to my normal everyday clothes. I walked out of the dojo just as others were arriving.

Dr Hatsumi's classes attract hundreds of students from all over the world. There were well over a hundred students there that day and I was going to have to face every one of them as I walked in the opposite direction. I nodded and smiled when I passed them, but there were no greetings or smiles back.

It was a hot day, the sun beating down. I walked out of the alley onto a road and stood to the side. I couldn't go back to the hotel because I had organised to meet Michiko Ohsaku, a writer, translator and great supporter of New Zealand children's books. We were meeting after my class and I had no way of contacting her. I was just going to have to wait.

While I stood there the steady stream of students on their way to class continued to pass by me. I greeted them with smiles, but there was still no reply. They were like soldiers on the way to the battlefield, each carrying a bag of weapons for the class.

I noticed a man beaming at me from an upstairs window of a Christian church across the street. He waved.

I gave a little wave back.

That's all I need, I thought. *Christians trying to convert me.* I looked away to avoid his attention.

I had only been in the sun for a short while and already I was starting to cook. As I watched the foreign students walk by I started to think that coming to Japan was a bad idea. I had reluctantly left my two kids back at home and my classes.

A wave caught my eye. The man from the church was now downstairs, smiling and waving to me from the door. I smiled and waved back. It was surreal. Hardened men were marching by, and here was this little man offering warmth and openness.

He walked out of the church, found his way around the serious students, and crossed the road to me.

'Are you okay?' he asked, sounding as though he hadn't used English for a little while.

'Yeah, I'm okay,' I replied, apprehensive about being converted or getting a sermon.

'It is very hot out here.' The man looked at the sky. 'Would you like an umbrella for the sun?'

'No, no, I'm okay,' I answered.

He asked me why I was standing out in the heat. I explained that I was waiting for a friend.

'Would you like to wait inside?' He gestured at the church.

'No, no, I'm okay,' I said again.

He left me and went back indoors.

As the stream of students began to dwindle some flash cars drove by. It was the top instructors, including Dr Hatsumi, who was being driven. The occupants of each car glanced at me as they passed. Then it was quiet.

There was a commotion at the church. I looked over to see that the man had brought others outside. They were all waving and smiling at me as they talked among themselves. They seemed to be concerned for my welfare.

'Would you like some water?' one person called out.

'I'm okay,' I said.

The original man came back over to me. 'When is your friend coming?'

I told him that my friend was two hours away.

'Come, come.' He beckoned. 'We have water for you.'

I decided to accept his generosity.

He took me across the road and into the church, where I was greeted individually by each member. They were families from the Philippines, working and living in Japan, and after sitting me down in front of a fan they gave me water and snacks. All of them were interested, wanting to know everything about me and about New Zealand, and they took photos with me. There was no preaching or converting. It was just like being with whānau. I felt as though the universe had put me exactly where I was supposed to be. I had found love in Japan. When Michiko arrived she got to meet my new friends.

The encounter reminded me of why I had moved on from combative arts and created Kura Toa and Warrior Kids. The contrast between the church and the martial arts school validated everything I had been trying to achieve through my classes. Kura Toa was a place of care and love.

SHAUN

One day, out of the blue, Shaun came to visit me at my flat in Henderson.

I had continued chasing after the family. Dad was now running his own lawn-mowing business and I had hooked him up with the owner of the flat to mow our lawns.

It was 1999 and Reed Publishing were about to release *The Wooden Fish* as its own book with my dedication in the front to Dad. That same year I had performed a mihi for Dad in a crowded restaurant and presented him with a pounamu for his birthday.

I was the same with Mum. I had taken a black-and-white photo of her, and had it enlarged and framed and hung it on my wall, and I'd been making regular trips down to visit her in Palmerston North.

For years I had been working hard to win my family over. I tried different approaches and kept changing myself into something that I hoped they could be proud of, but none of it worked. The harder I tried, the harder they pushed me away. It was all one-sided. When I eventually stopped phoning I never heard from them.

So it was a surprise to have my older brother turn up.

I made Shaun a hot drink and we sat in the lounge. Shaun and I chit-chatted for a little while and then he became serious. He started to tremble.

'You all right?' I asked.

Shaun began to cry.

'What's the matter, Shaun?' I queried, thinking my brother must have something big to tell me.

'I'm so proud of you,' he said. 'I'm just so proud of you.'

I didn't know what to say.

'You showed them—you showed them all.' Shaun wiped his eyes. 'They said you were a loser, that you wouldn't amount to anything. They called you a deadbeat. Uncle Todd, our cousins …' Shaun rattled off a list of Pākehā relatives and family acquaintances. 'They called you a no-hoper. They told me I shouldn't hang out with you because you'd just drag me down. They reckoned you were going to end up in trouble and in prison, but you proved them wrong.'

I sat there silent, taking it all in.

'Look at you now,' he said. 'You're an author. You created the Warrior Kids programme. You showed them, man. You showed them.'

It was a precious moment. This was the most real Shaun had been with me for a long time, and it never happened again. Following this I hardly ever saw or spoke to my older brother. I tried to keep up contact, but Mum wanted him to stay away from me.

Growing up in Shaun and Katie's positions in the family had been just as precarious as mine. At any point they could have ended up taking my place. Even Dad had to tread carefully.

There had been times when Mum had all of us assemble in the lounge. There she would make Dad stand in front of us kids, and we would have to vote on whether he could stay living with us or not. Dad would have to face each one of us as we cast our decision. It didn't matter what us kids voted, of course, because in the end Mum always had the final say. Really it was one of Mum's tactics to remind not just Dad, but all of us, who had the power.

To the wider family Shaun backed up Mum's rhetoric that I was bipolar and not okay in the head. When this failed, my siblings supported Mum in telling everyone that I had disowned my family and wanted nothing to do with them. It was all to explain why I wasn't around.

With the release of my books and the success of Warrior Kids the media wanted to know where I had come from and what had driven me to create them. Mum was very upset when I started being open to the public about the abuse and violence in my childhood. She talked to Uncle Blake, who was now living abroad. One evening I got a phone call.

'What's all these lies you've been telling people?' Uncle Blake asked. 'It's all bullshit! Nothing bad happened to you!'

I stayed quiet.

'You'd better shut your mouth, boy,' he said, 'or I'll be over there to shut it for you!'

With interviews of me talking about my past appearing in print and on screen it was said that I was taking out my anger on Mum and Dad. That I was abusing my parents by shaming them. This was Mum's narrative, and Shaun and Katie had to go along with it or end up being cast adrift as well.

Many of the wider family were happy to go along with it too because the truth was too close to home and much harder to live with. There is great deal of shame throughout the family about the generational abuse and violence. They would prefer that the past remains swept beneath the carpet. There are too many implications for many of them.

'It was your own fault that you got hurt,' Shaun would say. 'You were always there—that's why Dad and Mum went for you. You should have been quiet like me, and stayed in your bedroom.'

I would say now that I was the lucky one out of us kids, because I was rejected and cast out of the family. Shaun became locked into an enmeshed, co-dependant relationship with Mum where he didn't know where he began and she ended. The threat of losing her love and approval was ever-present for Shaun. Mum played head games with him and manipulated him throughout his childhood, through his teens and even well into his adult years. She held her love, her affection and later her money on the end of a string, forever having him chase her. She interfered with every part of his life.

Shaun had enormous pressure on him to achieve at school. Mum would have him in tears if he wasn't doing right. She directed his relationships and his jobs. Shaun gave up his dreams and himself to dutifully follow Mum's every bidding.

No one could ever tell Shaun that though. No one could challenge Mum either, or call her to account, because Shaun would be there, standing in front of her. Shaun was her defender, forever making excuses and justifying Mum's behaviour and demanding that everyone leave her alone. As far as Shaun was concerned, I was the bad one for having made Mum's life so difficult.

Just as it was for Katie, the abuse Shaun endured was largely overshadowed by the extremity of my abuse, and they have both said that our family's past is simply too shameful to think of.

A LOVE STORY
part one

One evening in 2004 I stopped at my usual Chinese takeaway on Swanson Road to get some dinner. When I walked in to order a Chinese woman looked up from the deep fryers behind the counter. Our eyes met and we shared a smile. I hadn't seen this woman here before. She carried on cooking and I made my order, yet our eyes kept finding one another.

When she came close to the counter I asked her if she had just started working here. She wasn't confident in speaking English and struggled to reply.

The manager of the store came over with his nephew. I thought that they might help the woman and I communicate. I was wrong. The two men told me to go away and to leave the woman alone. I would find out later that the manager was hoping that the woman would marry his nephew.

I got my food and walked out deflated. Used to disappointment I shrugged it off. As I drove home I tried to forget all about the mysterious woman. Clearly she wasn't for me.

A month later I pulled up at the takeaway shop again to get some dinner. I was about to walk in when the woman came bounding out the door.

'Hello,' she smiled.

She had just finished her shift and was heading home. However now she was wanting to talk to me and there was no one to stop us this time. Even though the woman felt uncomfortable using English she gave it a good go. She told me that her name was Rebecca. I felt that that was an unusual name for someone who had been born in mainland China. I gave Rebecca my phone number and she got in her car and left. I had enjoyed our talk, yet I figured that I probably wouldn't hear from her.

A couple of days later Rebecca texted. She wanted me to meet her in the carpark outside her work one afternoon. When we met we sat in her car and talked.

I was 32 and she was 29.

'Where did you get the name Rebecca from?' I asked.

She explained to me that she had worked for a western company in Beijing, and that the western companies in China get their employees to adopt western names as they are easier for westerners to accept and pronounce.

'What is your Chinese name?' I asked.

'Ping,' she said.

'Ping is easier to pronounce than Rebecca,' I replied.

'But Ping is an unusual name for westerners.'

'Not for me, I'm not going to call you Rebecca. Your name is Ping so I'm going to call you Ping.'

People had always had trouble pronouncing Tipene and because of this I had put a great deal of effort in insuring that I respected and pronounced other people's names.

I saw Ping again after that, and again. Each time we met I expected it to be our last. Ping was beautiful on the outside and inside. She was a kind and genuine person. I didn't think that someone like her could be interested in someone like me, especially long term.

When Ping went back to see her family in Beijing I just assumed that my time with her was over and that I wouldn't see her again. I was wrong. She phoned me from China regularly and in the end she even cut her visit short because she was missing me so much.

I was perplexed by Ping because she wasn't like anyone I had ever dated before. It was the little things that turned out to be big things for me.

One afternoon we were lying on the bed together, asleep. Feeling Ping stir, my hypervigilance kicked in. Alert I laid still with my eyes closed but was aware of Ping getting up. She started to head out of the bedroom, but she stopped on my side of the bed. I was conscious of her standing over me. Accustomed to expecting the worse my body tensed up with anticipation that I was going to have to protect myself.

Ping pulled the blankets over me and tucked me in. She then left the room, quietly pulling the door closed behind her.

Alone, I opened my eyes. I was confused. No one had ever tucked me in before. Who was this woman? It was summer and I was hot under those blankets, however I didn't want to move.

On one of our first dates Ping took me to a Chinese restaurant in town. It was my introduction to Yum Cha, a southern Chinese custom of eating small servings of different food while sipping Chinese tea. I drove us to the restaurant. During the drive Ping reached over from the passenger seat and touched the back of my neck with her hand.

'What are you doing?' I flinched.

'Oh sorry,' thinking that she had breached some cultural protocol, Ping quickly withdrew her hand.

I looked at her.

'What were you doing?'

'I was just going to rub your neck,' she replied.

'Why?'

'I'm sorry, I won't do it again.'

'No, no,' I answered, trying to reassure her. 'Don't be sorry, I just didn't know what you were doing. Show me again.'

Ping placed her hand on the back of my neck and gently massaged. The reaction was immediate. I felt my body give and soften. Ping's tenderness was soothing, but it was also frightening. I wasn't used to it. I felt emotional like I was going to cry. However as much as the touch made me feel uncomfortable I didn't want Ping to stop.

Ping was consistently nice towards me. There were no dramas and no expectations. She never complained or criticised me and she didn't want me to change.

It was easy. Too easy. We just seemed to fit. Something had to be wrong. This couldn't be right. I figured that the relationship wasn't going to last. There was no way that someone as wonderful as Ping was going to put up with me and all of my baggage.

However as far as Ping was concerned, her and I were supposed to be together. She was convinced that everything would work out. She had even convinced her family that I was some great guy.

I tried to get her to see reason. I told her all about my past. She didn't really understand.

I explained to Ping that I had no money and that I didn't own a house. I was a poor writer. I had created the Warrior Kids program for children, but there was no money in it. I echoed the multitude of complaints from past girlfriends. I wasn't a good choice. I was high maintenance, a lot of work with few prospects. I was a bad bet.

'In China most writers are poor,' she said. 'I don't care.'

Who was this woman, and why was she being so unreasonable? She was doing my head in.

I told myself that Ping was obviously suffering from low self-esteem and didn't believe that she could find anyone better to be with. However Ping had other options, men would often try and talk to her, but she wasn't interested in them.

I told her about my promiscuity.

'If you're going to sleep with someone else that's fine,' she said. 'Just be safe and come home to me. Don't let any woman take advantage and use you. Choose someone who is nice to you.'

Now I knew that Ping wasn't right in the head. Who in their right mind would say something like that?

But Ping was sincere, she meant what she was saying. Her words hit me like a thunderbolt and, like some spell, the lasting effects of those words changed my life forever. No one had ever said these words to me and they became instrumental in changing my compulsive behaviour. Suddenly going elsewhere lost all of its power.

Ping didn't care that I was poor, that I had been abused, that I was struggling to hold it all together. She didn't care about any of that. She simply wanted to be with me.

Ping was becoming my safe place and that was the only place I wanted to be. It was a place where I was comforted, loved and accepted just for being me.

The problem was I had no idea how to be with unconditional love. I didn't know how to be close to someone who wasn't abusive to me and how to be in a relationship where I wasn't wrong. Although I had had psychotherapy and done a great deal of work on myself and changed my life, I still expected the worst. I tried to be positive. I read books on it, had positive mantras and affirmations that I said over and over every day, however I was conditioned to presume that everything would end bad for me. I believed that bad was all I deserved.

HERE COMES THE SUN

When Ping became pregnant in 2005 I just assumed that the baby would be aborted like all the others babies in my life. In the past when other women had become pregnant there had always been a discussion. I was always asked what I wanted, yet the decision for termination had already been decided. It was just a matter of convincing me. I was expected to go with what the woman wanted and not to cause a fuss and give her a hard time. I was there for her. To stand by her and support her.

This time though Ping didn't bring abortion up, so I asked her outright. She was horrified that I would even suggest such a thing. She was over the moon that she was pregnant with me. As far as she was concerned we were keeping the baby. We were going to be a family.

I was overwhelmed with thoughts and emotions. There was joy and love, there was amazement and perplexation, and there was fear and anxiety.

I was convinced that Ping was making a mistake in choosing to be with me. I was the wrong choice. Someone who had a proper career would be able to look after her and the baby. Someone who wasn't as damaged as me.

When I wasn't running Warrior Kids in schools I was waiting for Ping to finish work. The pregnancy was exciting and scary for the both of us. We didn't have any money to go out so we mostly stayed in the one bedroom that Ping had been renting in Ranui, West Auckland.

It was here that I wrote my story Hinemoa te toa as Ping laid back on the bed with an enormous belly. At this point we were nearing due date and so we were just waiting around for baby to arrive. When I write I tend to act out my stories, pacing about and getting into each of the characters, and so I excitedly performed my new story for Ping over and over. She would just lay there, rubbing her belly and watching me. I think she got a little tired of the story in the end.

Hinemoa te toa tells the story of a tough and brave little girl.

'I am a warrior,' she'd say, 'Hinemoa te toa - just like my ancestors.'

It's clear to see that Ping, who was so far away from her home and family in China and setting up a life here in NZ, was an inspiration. My sister Katie was also an inspiration, along with my aunties and cousins in the whanau. The girls and women in my life had all been tough and brave, including Mum.

In that bedroom Ping and I talked a lot. As Mandarin was Ping's first language and English was mine, we often resorted to using a translation dictionary to help with the communication and the understanding of certain words. There were times when we misunderstood one another. One afternoon Ping knocked a bowl of food over in the bedroom. It made a mess and Ping started saying how useless she was.

As far as I was concerned Ping was the most amazing woman I had ever met. I never liked hearing her complain and be hard on herself, so as usual I told her to stop it and I reassured her.

Ping started to cry.

'Don't say that, You always say that.'

'Eh?'

'You always say that,' Ping said.

'What? You mean, stop it?'

'Yes, you always call me stop it.'

I was confused.

'You always call me stop it,' she reiterated.

Suddenly I realised what she was meaning.

'No, no, no,' I gasped. 'I didn't say stupid.'

Ping frowned.

I got a piece of paper and wrote 'stop it' in large letters.

'This is what I said,' I explained. 'I have never called you stupid. I would never call you that.'

'Oh,' Ping laughed. 'I thought that you were always calling me stupid.'

I was horrified. I had been telling Ping to 'stop it' for months.

BEIJING WATERMELON

Ping couldn't understand my family. Especially when we went to the birthing unit at Waitakere hospital alone early in 2006 to have a baby. Ping couldn't understand how my mother would choose to stay away from her son, especially at an important time like this.

Ping wanted the birth of our child to be natural. She didn't want to have any drugs. That changed however on the day. It was a long labour and the birth went haywire. Ping had drugs and was barely conscious through the whole ordeal.

At one point the doctor said that he required consent for an epidural to be injected into Ping's spine. I didn't think Ping was in any state to make a decision like that. The doctor obviously thought the same, as he looked directly at me and started to explain the procedure. The mid-wife and nurse were coaching a mumbling Ping as I leaned against the bed listening to the doctor. I tried to take in what he was saying, but I was riddled with so much fear and anxiety that I could only nod and watch his mouth move. However when the doctor mentioned that there was the risk that Ping may never walk again and that there was even a risk of death I woke up.

'Sorry,' I said. 'Could you say that again.'

The doctor told me that there was a chance that Ping could die, a chance that it could be the baby that died, and even a chance that both mother and baby could die; and that was with the epidural and without it.

'We're heading into complications,' the Doctor said, handing me a consent form and a pen. 'We're obligated to explain the risks.'

Suddenly Ping's life and the life of our baby was in my hands. I was responsible for both of them and the doctor wanted me to sign off on it right then and there.

He seemed to think that the epidural was the way to go. Ping hadn't wanted any drugs, but now she was having everything. There was no time to think.

'Please God,' I pleaded as I signed the form.

Ping had the epidural injection and then everything started to speed up. The umbilical chord was wrapped around baby's neck. Baby had to come out and come out now. Ping roused and begged the doctor for a caesarean. She had had enough.

The doctor wasn't having that.

'We don't do that here,' he said. 'This is not China.'

At the time caesarean births were common practise in Beijing and there were a number of different reasons why Chinese women felt pressured to have them. Natural births were preferred in New Zealand. Caesareans were only used as a very last resort.

Ping was exhausted. The midwife, the nurse, the doctor and myself all got around her and got her to push. I had spent the entire labour focussed on Ping and trying to help and support her through. I could feel my own body as well though. I had never experienced so much tension before. I was starting to question how much more my body could take. I didn't want to suddenly keel over which is what I felt I was about to do. Forceps were used and a baby boy was born weighing over 8 pounds.

Ping wanted me to name our baby. I named him Taiyang which mean Sun in Mandarin. He was now a light in my life.

Holding our new born son I wasn't excited. I was relieved. I was relieved that Ping and baby were both alive. I kept watching the medical staff as they were busy around us. I studied their faces, still fearful that something could go wrong. When I wasn't worrying about that, I was worrying about the future and how I was going to look after my family.

The nurse asked Ping if she wanted a shower. Ping's family had a tradition of the women not showering for a month after giving birth for fear of infection and other complications during the harsh winters in China. Ping had planned to stick to that tradition. However now she couldn't get into the shower quick enough.

Once her and baby were asleep I went home. The next day I cooked Chicken soup, another Chinese tradition for mothers after a birth, and took it into Ping.

I could see the light in my new born son straight away, his unique individual spirit. It was wonderful to meet him and to know that our futures were tied together. I was out to be the best father in the world. I now had even more incentive to stay alive and address my past.

Our lack of family support in New Zealand concerned the midwife and nurse at the hospital. They and Plunket were even concerned at one point that Ping might be suffering from postnatal depression. But it was really that Ping and I didn't have a clue. Neither of us were confident in being a parent or in being in a relationship.

¤ ¤ ¤

When Taiyang was 6 months old Ping and I took him to Beijing. It was time for he and I to meet Ping's family. I was nervous and my hypervigilance was spiralling. I would be on their turf, in their space, and have nowhere to retreat to. Ping's family couldn't speak English and I couldn't speak Mandarin. At the time I was a poor author and a Warrior Kids instructor who owned nothing. I was sure I wasn't going to be good enough for Ping's family. I certainly hadn't been good enough for my own family and for the families of past girlfriends. I was expecting the worse.

When we arrived at the apartment Ping was in demand, with everyone in her family wanting to talk to her. Taking another phone call from yet another aunty, Ping left the room, while I stayed at the dining table with some of her other relatives. The relatives kept trying to talk to me in Mandarin and all I could do in reply was shrug and give an expression that I didn't understand.

Ma, Ping's mother, proudly produced a large watermelon. Ma had brought it from the markets especially for our arrival and to welcome me to Beijing. It was a hot day and the watermelon looked delicious. However, prior to leaving Auckland I had looked into the recommended food-safety requirements for New Zealanders travelling to China. It was strongly advised that Kiwis drink only bottled water and eat only cooked fruit and vegetables. I was certain that as good as that watermelon might look, it wasn't going to be good for me at all.

Ma smiled at me, took a large knife and sliced the watermelon open. I looked about for Ping, but she was in another room with the door shut.

Ma gestured at me and the watermelon as she sliced it up. It was obvious the raw fruit was coming my way.

'Ping!' I called.

There was no reply.

Ma took the biggest slice of watermelon and offered it to me from across the table.

'Bu yao,' I said, knowing it meant *I don't want* in Mandarin. It was one of the phrases that Ping had been teaching me.

Ma wasn't taking no for an answer. 'Chi, chi,' she said, telling me to eat as she started to make her way around the table, while holding out the piece of watermelon.

'Ping!' I cried.

I could hear Ping talking on the phone, but she wasn't answering me.

'Chi, chi, chi,' Ma kept saying as she closed in.

'Ping!'

Ma came up on me so I leaned right back in my seat, trying to get as far away from the watermelon as I could.

'Chi, chi, chi,' Ma said, standing right over me as though I were an infant.

'Bu yao, bu yao,' I replied. 'Ping!'

Ma placed a hand on the back of my head and pulled me forward while forcing the slice of watermelon into my mouth with her other hand.

It tasted delicious.

Ping eventually emerged from the other room. She looked at Ma standing over me, hand-feeding me slices of watermelon.

'You're not supposed to be eating that,' Ping said.

'I know,' I said.

Watermelon was just the beginning. During my stay in Beijing, Ma was putting food in front of me every chance that she got. Dumplings, noodles, Chinese stews, and I was expected to eat it all. Ma made sure that I had money when I went out, that I had everything that I needed and more. A master of Tai Chi Ma even took it upon herself to teach me.

I was blessed with whānau as a kid—aunties and uncles treated me as their nephew, and I can only say good things about my grandparents—but I never knew motherly love until I met Ma. As far as Ma and the rest of the relatives were concerned I was now a part of the family.

Ping and I had a baby together, so in their eyes we were married. Ma even presented us with the traditional marriage blankets signifying our union. They were heavy blankets suitable for Beijing winter. Mine was covered with red silk on the top with a pair of embroidered dragons. Ping's was covered with blue silk with a pair of phoenix. They were beautiful.

With all of Ma's generosity I wasn't allowed to say thank you. Every time I said thank you Ma would get upset. In Ping's culture you only say thank you to strangers, never to family. Every time I said thank you to Ma I was saying that she was a stranger to me. In her eyes it meant that I wasn't accepting her as mother in-law. So she worked harder to try and please me.

'But Ma is the number one person that I should be saying thank you to,' I said to Ping. 'She is more important than any stranger and I want her to know that I value and appreciate all that she is doing for me.'

'Ma just wants you to accept it,' Ping explained.

What followed was a game of Ma looking after me and each time me saying, 'thank you, I mean no, no thank you.' There were a lot of laughs, but I got there in the end.

¤ ¤ ¤

I did get sick in Beijing, but it had nothing to do with the food. I was spinning out of control. It was just like when I had started working at Mt Tabor, but this time only worse. I was having to be a part of a loving and warm family and I didn't know how. The pot had been stirred and all of my past was coming to the surface. I was riddled with anxiety and my body was wound up tight. It was excruciating. I was like a caged wild animal.

Ping was encouraging me to relax, but I didn't know how. I tried breathing exercises, went for walks yet nothing would settle the storm raging within me. The more effort the family put in to including me and the more Ma mothered me, the more I withdrew into myself. It was all just too much. I went into overload. The family didn't understand what was going on. We couldn't speak each other's language. They tried to carry on like normal, proudly introducing Taiyang and me to all the relatives, neighbours and even the odd person walking down the street. At times I would simply shut down. Ping said that I was coming across uninterested and rude, like I didn't want to be there. That was the last impression that I wanted to give. I tried to talk to Ping about what was going on for me, but I couldn't get my head around it, let alone find the adequate words in translation. I was running on emotions, thick in hypervigilance. I was in fight or flight mode. I wanted to run away, but I didn't have anywhere to run. Poor Ping had no idea what I was going through. As much as I tried to explain it to her, she just took my manner and withdrawn behaviour as a sign that I didn't want to be with her, and that I couldn't handle the relationship.

'I don't want to do this anymore,' she said. 'I want us to separate and just be friends.'

Ping thought that by saying this it would make the demons go away, that the pressure would then be off me and I could relax. However the gate to hell had already been opened. I hadn't been easy to live with before, but now I was worse. I became obsessed with trying to give Taiyang the perfect life. I was determined that he would never have a life like mine. Ping wasn't a confident mother and I only made it worse by putting so much pressure on the both of us.

There was much that I did enjoy about my trip to China, yet I would have enjoyed it a great deal more if I had been able to relax.

DADDY'S GIRL

After being away together, and being so welcomed and accepted by her family, I felt closer to Ping. But it was all unravelling.

Back in New Zealand Ping and I tried to continue living together, but it wasn't long and we were apart. Taiyang and I rented a room at a friend's place. I was full time parent. Ping didn't feel confident to parent on her own. It was a hard time for all of us. Ping went back to work and I ended up having to go on the Domestic Services Benefit. I hated it.

Ping and I were still close though and she soon fell pregnant again.

I found a new place for Ping, Taiyang and I to live together again.

Ping's parents, Ma and Ba, visited New Zealand. They arrived near the end of 2007 for the birth of our second child.

This time Ping and I didn't go to Waitakere hospital alone. Ma came with us. Unlike the first birth the second one was a lot easier. Ma was worried though. During the labour she dropped to her knees beside Ping's bed and started prostrating to Buddha, muttering prayers in mandarin.

The midwife looked at me.

'Could you get her out of the way please,' she said.

I got Ma up, made sure that she was okay then went back to looking after Ping.

Unlike her brother who seemed to have wanted to stay in the womb, our daughter was in a rush to get out. When she emerged she was full of life. She cried in the nurse's hands so she was passed to Ping. She still cried. Ping passed her to Ma. The baby wouldn't stop crying.

'Give her to Tim,' Ping said.

I took hold of my daughter, said hello and she stopped crying and looked up at me. That's when I started crying.

Everyone laughed.

'Daddy's girl,' the nurse said.

I had spoken to our daughter when she was in the womb, just as I had done with Taiyang. She knew my voice.

Ping wanted me to give our daughter a western name. She felt that our mixed children wouldn't be so accepted in New Zealand and that the racism would be hard enough as it was, so I named her Tahlia. But I also wanted another name representing light so I gave her a middle name, Yueyue, meaning moon in mandarin. My life was a lot brighter now.

¤ ¤ ¤

When it was just the two of us, just me and Ping, it was much easier. We only had to worry about ourselves and one another. When the babies came along Ping's self-doubt emerged.

She even believed that her breast milk was inadequate to feed the babies. It took some convincing for her to think otherwise.

There was a reason Ping had chosen to live on the other side of the world. Her father was a doctor, her mother and sister both nurses. Ping wasn't either of these things. There is enormous pressure in China and Ping believed that she wasn't good enough.

I didn't help. I was emotionally all over the place. I was trying to provide for my family, yet wasn't bringing in enough money for us to live on. At the same time I was trying to be in relationship with Ping and parent Taiyang and Tahlia, when I didn't know how to do either. We had no money. Ping was constantly worrying where our next meal was coming from and how we were going to pay the bills.

Over tired, Ping would numb out at times as though she was in another world. Plunket were concerned. They tried to get Ping into a Chinese support group, but she refused to go.

In hindsight what I should have done was look after Ping more. I should have been there encouraging and supporting her. The last thing Ping needed was more criticism. She already had people criticising her. There were times where I was supportive, however the times when I was critical had the greater impact, and the criticism was simply a reflection of my own doubt and lack of self-belief. It actually had nothing to do with Ping at all, but I wasn't seeing that at the time.

For Ping it must have felt like the whole world was against her and that she could do nothing right. I should have been the one person to have her back, and I wasn't. It got to the point where Ping believed that she wasn't good enough to be a mother and a partner.

¤ ¤ ¤

Ping left me.

She packed her bags and walked out on me and the kids just before Christmas 2008. She had been at me about leaving for weeks, saying that she had had enough and that she wanted to go. Previously I had managed to talk her out of it, but in the end I could only stand there, holding our two babies and watching her go. and hoping she would turn back. She didn't.

I was devastated, but I wasn't surprized. This was my life, and my life had always been turmoil and drama. I had struggled from the day I was born, why should it stop now.

In order to avoid the benefit I tried to increase the number of Warrior Kids classes that I was doing. However, the amount I could do was limited due to now being a full time parent of a one year old girl and a boy who was nearly three. Ping agreed to look after the babies for the few hours that I was running classes as long as it didn't clash with her work. Outside of that I had the babies seven days and nights a week.

I was angry at Ping. Angry that she had left Taiyang and Tahlia. Angry that she had left me. Angry that I had to go it alone and turn to WINZ. I felt so hurt and rejected.

Ping had left because she believed that she was a bad parent. She didn't think she was good enough to be a mother.

In leaving me and the babies she copped even more criticism. For her it fulfilled the belief that she wasn't enough, and through the rejection of her going it did the same for me. We were perpetuating our own realities. We both made it happen, we were both responsible. As much as Ping had chosen to leave, I had pushed her out.

What was really sad was that beneath the anger and hurt we still really loved one another, and we both loved our kids.

A GOOD FATHER

People had often commented throughout my life that I was a patient person. I had thought that I was a patient person too, until I was on my own with two babies.

No longer able to rent the house that Ping and I had been living in together I was now in desperate need of a place to stay. I ended up renting a room from an ex girlfiend for me and my children. I was still running the odd Warrior Kids class when I could, however there was very little writing being done during this time. Any ideas for stories was lost in the constant demands from the children. My life was changing nappies, cooking, bathing, cleaning, playing, reading stories, getting the kids off to sleep and then doing it all over again.

I became sleep deprived and much of what was happening each day in those early years of my children's lives was just a blur. There were days where I was taking my kids out in public with their clothes inside out or on backwards. It was the disapproval in the eyes of onlookers that brought these mishaps to my attention.

In the world of kids there was an endless amount of birthday parties and I made sure Taiyang and Tahlia attended all that they were invited to. I went all out when it was their special days too. I got quite good at playing host and making birthday cakes. It was a lot of work, but also a lot of fun.

Ping often wouldn't attend the birthday parties though I would go to great lengths to try and get her there. It was understandable though. She was embarrassed. It was as though she was a guest at her own child's birthday party, a party that I had put together with the help of my ex-girlfriend.

Taiyang and Tahlia were always upset when their mother didn't show. Ping would try and make amends after each party, buying another cake, an expensive gift and cooking an amazing meal. Ping is an incredible cook. I am a good cook too, and have been the main cook in my children's lives, but Taiyang and Tahlia see their mother as the master chef, and I agree.

'I want to be a woman when I grow up,' Taiyang said to me when he was six.

'Why do you want to be a woman?' I asked.

'Women have more fun,' he said. 'Men just cook, clean and do house work.'

This was Taiyang's reality. In his world I was the main caregiver. I gave my life to my kids. Having a life outside of them was impossible.

In China when a spouse leaves the home they can lose all rights to the children. Ping knew that that wasn't the case in New Zealand. She knew that she had every right to have the children stay with her, but she preferred spending time with me and the kids together.

Ping and I talked often about getting back together, yet whenever I tried to make it happen Ping changed her mind. She was fearful that it would end up the same as it had the last time.

I started to think that I needed to let go of her and move on.

I was led to believe that women like a man with children. I found out that that's not true. While I had relationships with single mum's when I was on my own, I couldn't find any woman who was willing to have a relationship with me as a single dad. Dates would go well until I mentioned that my kids lived with me. At least the women were upfront about not wanting to raise another women's children.

¤ ¤ ¤

My compulsive promiscuous behaviour was never the same after Ping had entered my life. She had shown me that I was worthy of love and that I needed to be safe with who I let in. Ping was still out to protect me, telling me that if I was going to find someone else then I needed to choose someone nice.

Promiscuity had always brought dramas and I didn't want any of that near my kids, and nor did I want them to think that that sort of behaviour was normal and okay. I didn't want them following in my footsteps. I knew that my role as a parent was to lead by example. I loved being a father and I had to look my children in the eyes every day, and I wanted to be able to do so with a clear conscience.

While at times I resented being on my own with two kids, I was very thankful that I had this opportunity to be a hands on parent. It enabled me to grow into a much fuller individual. I was also grateful for the years of running Warrior Kids because now I was putting all that I had learnt and taught into practice, and it was paying off.

I was getting to redesign my own childhood each and every day. I read to my kids. No one had read to me when I was a child. When my children made a mistake I sat down and talked with them about it. I didn't give them a hiding or a smack. When a parent informed me that my six year old boy was copying other kids and using bad words at school I drove straight to the school, took him aside in his classroom and calmly spoke to him about it. I didn't think that he was being a 'little shit'. I saw my boy as the child that he was, needing my love and guidance.

I wasn't ready for either of my kids to go to Kindy or to School, but both of them couldn't wait to get there. While they bounded in with smiles and enthusiasm, I retreated to the car and wept.

When it came to education I didn't force or push my kids. I simply believed in them, encouraged and praised their attempts, and in return they showed that they were both self-directed learners. They became avid readers, would do all sorts of art and science projects around the home, and do maths just for fun. Living in a safe and happy home my kids excelled.

When Taiyang was four he came outside one afternoon to where I was taking a moment out of the day to watch the natural world around me—the breeze pushing through the branches of the trees, the flowers in the garden, and the birds and the insects all full of life. Taiyang began jumping and waving his arms about.

'Uh,' he tutted. 'Why can't I fly like a butterfly.'

It was a beautiful moment, and there have been a multitude of these moments that I got to share with my children. I felt sad that Ping was missing out on them. My children are miracles that continue to bless my life. Out of all my achievements my greatest was in being a good father.

A LOVE STORY
Part two

In 2015 my kids and I visited my cousin, Allan, and his partner, Pete, in their apartment in the city. We had a wonderful evening. However Allan and Pete's apartment was near the top floor of a high building, and when I went out on to the balcony I suddenly had an overwhelming and uncontrollable urge to jump. I looked around at Taiyang and Tahlia. Suicide had come up frequently over the years but I had no desire to end my life now. I had chosen to live for my kids, yet my mind was transfixed on leaping off the side of the building. I couldn't get it out of my head. I went back inside the apartment and stayed away from the balcony.

When I got home I assumed that it had been a onetime thing and shrugged it off. This wasn't the case. I visited my cousin a number of times in his apartment and the impulse to jump only got louder. It got to a point where I was dreading going there. I knew then that something was wrong and that I needed help.

I have gone through periods of therapy a number of times in my life to address the past, and now I knew that it was time to return to it. My original psychotherapist, Glenn, had always been amazed at how much I was willing to push and challenge myself. For me it was a testament of how bad I felt inside and how much I wanted a better life.

Previous therapists had informed me that I was entitled to ACC funding due to the sexual abuse that I had experienced. ACC will only fund historical cases of childhood sexual abuse which have resulted in the individual experiencing adult Post-Traumatic Stress Disorder. They will not fund historical cases of physical or emotional abuse even though they also produce PTSD in adults. This is solely because PTSD as a result of childhood sexual abuse is included in the DSM (Diagnostic and Statistical Manual of Mental

Disorders), but other forms of Developmental Traumas are not. It was weird to feel relief over the fact that I had been sexually abused but it meant that I could get my therapy paid for.

Not wanting to waste the opportunity I had held off allowing a therapist to access my ACC funding until I had found the right one.

At the beginning of 2016 I met a therapist named Anne. Anne had long heard of me and my work in the community. She had also worked with agencies that I had taken referrals from in the past with Warrior Kids.

Therapy isn't easy. One has to have courage and commitment to see it through. I've had some very low and scary times. My therapy involved EMDR, or Eye movement desensitization and reprocessing which is a form of psychotherapy developed in 1988 to treat PTSD.

After my first year with Anne, I received a call from an ACC case worker to see how my therapy was going. I broke down in tears over the phone. I was just so thankful. I told him that because of that funding ACC had saved my life. Without it there was a slim chance that I would be alive today. The uncontrollable urge to end my life had gotten that bad.

I had addressed the violence of my childhood, the emotional, psychological and physical abuse, but I had only touched on the sexual abuse. Now I was having to face and work through it. The impact of childhood trauma is long lasting.

¤ ¤ ¤

'Ping loves you, Tim,' Anne said during a session.

I just sat there taking it in.

'Ping didn't move on, she didn't start a new relationship,' Anne continued. 'She is still there for you and the kids.'

I realised that I hadn't been able to see beyond my anger. I was holding on to the fact that Ping had walked out on me and the kids, and holding it against her.

The reason that Ping and I had gotten on so well was because underneath it all we were very similar. It was the same reason why we had ended up apart. Ping believed that she wasn't good enough to be a mother and a partner. She believed that her children and I would be better off without her. There was no question of her love. It was obvious that Ping loved us. She was always spoiling us and cooking wonderful meals. Her and I had never stopped being close to one another. Even when I had tried to move on with another woman.

The other side of this was that I wasn't allowing myself to have something good, wonderful and honest. I wasn't allowing myself to be loved. I was still believing that I wasn't worthy of love.

That morning with Anne a switch had been flicked. I felt ashamed of how I had treated Ping—the one and only person who had stuck by me through thick and thin. Sure she had let me down at times, but her love had never faulted. It had remained steadfast and true. From that point on I just enjoyed each moment that I had with Ping. I praised and supported her. Naturally we fell together as though we had never been apart. It was simple and easy. Ping wasn't sure for a while. She kept questioning me, testing to see if I was going to change my mind—if I was going to turn around at some point and say that it wasn't working or criticize her, but I didn't and Ping started to relax more and more. So much so that early in 2017 she moved in to live with me and the kids. I had been a single parent for eight years and now we were back together as family. Taiyang and Tahlia were so happy. People were commenting on how much they were beaming. It was nothing short of a miracle.

After so many years Ping and I know each other so well. Ping and I have spoken of the past and our actions, and we are gentle with ourselves and with each other, knowing that through our hard times we had still loved one another, and that it was only our self-loathing, doubts and past hurts that had kept us apart. We have been living together for over three years now and we haven't looked back. I adore and love Ping with all my heart, and know that I always have.

'Yours is a romance story, Tim,' Anne said. 'It has a happy ending.'

LIFE IS GOOD

I love my Mum and Dad. It might be hard to believe that, considering what I have written about them. Yet rather than sugar-coat and soften my story, I wanted to say it just as it was for me. After years of not wanting to see the harsh reality, I've had to in order to accept and move on from it.

I understand the trajectory of my parents' lives, the cause and effect. Life is complex, and the deeper Mum and Dad dug themselves into the lives they chose to live, the harder it was for them to come out of it. How could my parents face and own what they did to me? How could anyone?

Now my life is far removed from the violence and abuse I grew up with. It wasn't easy though. There have been lots of ups and downs, bouts of depression and failures. There were other relationships, periods of homelessness, lots of therapy.

And Warrior Kids often took more than it gave.

In the early days I contracted an accountant because I wanted to ensure I followed the IRD rules. However after a few years he challenged me.

'It's not a business,' he said, 'and it's not a charity because you don't accept donations or receive funding. Financially the running costs far exceed any profit. The fact is, Tim, it has never made money, so we've now listed it as a hobby.'

Struggling as I was, I didn't mind too much. I had always wanted to run a professional service, but it had never been about making money for me.

There were attempts by some to take the programme from me. Others just tried to duplicate it. Frustration, resentment, anxiety, grief, depression, anger and burn-out—I've felt it all with Warrior Kids. There were times I tried to pack it in and walk away. However families, schools and organisations kept begging me to continue and so I would soldier on, and I'm glad I did.

I have now been running Warrior Kids for 26 years. In that time I have worked with thousands of children and their families in schools and communities.

There have been numerous publicised accounts from ex-students and parents about how much Warrior Kids and I changed their lives, as well as positive reviews from schools and organisations. I achieved what I set out to do. My teenage dream of having a full time space for my classes came true. In 2009 Kura Toa Warrior School was opened by then Mayor of Waitakere, Sir Bob Harvey, in Ranui, West Auckland. I managed to pay the lease through running classes.

I proved that one person could make a difference.

When I first started my programme for children I had no qualifications other than my black belts in the martial arts. Yet I went on to gain certificates in counselling and a graduate certificate in Child and Adolescent Mental Health. I pursued further grades in the martial arts because I never felt I had enough credentials; however it was the response from outside my martial arts that showed me I had more than enough.

Warrior Kids and I were featured on television, and there have been articles in magazines and newspapers. In Japan I met with world-renowned Kodansha International Publishers, and in China with officials from Tsinghua University in Beijing—just because they wanted to know what Warrior Kids was all about and to see how I had adapted martial arts for children and teenagers in New Zealand. They wanted to know how my ideas might work for them.

There have been awards. In 2013 I was inducted into the New Zealand Martial Arts Hall of Fame, and in 2014 I was recognised as a Kiwibank New Zealander of the year Local Hero. I was also getting books published. Yet there were times when I wanted to give up writing. It was never nice to see my books relegated to the back of bookstores—that's if they made it into the stores in the first place, because there were some that didn't. It was frustrating to be told that as Māori books they were a niché market and didn't warrant as much publicity and attention. Yet after 24 years I am now an award-winning Māori author, with eleven books published and more on the way. Not bad for someone who was kicked out of school.

After *The Wooden Fish* came out in 1999 I started being asked to speak in schools. Today I am an inspirational speaker to audiences both young and old, sharing my story of how I overcame a violent and abusive childhood, and after twenty years I think I'm getting quite good at it.

Ping, Taiyang, Tahlia and I are happy. Our family is whole again. With help from our family in China we were able to get a deposit for a home and I found one with a large garage which I have turned into a studio for my classes.

Ping's family have known me for sixteen years now and they cannot understand how my parents choose not to have anything to do with their son and their grandchildren. They regard me as an orphan. It was the only way that they could explain why my parents weren't involved in my life. Some of Ping's relatives had even taken it upon themselves to coach me on how to be in a family.

It seems that I have been adopted twice in my life—first by a Māori family, and the second time by a Chinese family, one who now treat me as their own. What can I say? I feel extremely blessed.

A couple of years ago I was preparing to leave on another author tour when Ma asked to speak to me over a video call. She has been learning English and wanted to send me off with a blessing.

'Tim,' she said. 'Expect everything to be good.'

Her words hit me directly in the heart.

'Wow, that's beautiful,' I said.

Ping waved it off.

'She says that sort of thing all the time,'

Ma's words have stayed with me and I keep coming back to them.

I have accomplished a lot in my life, and there is more I am set on achieving. And I expect it all to be good.

TO THE READER

Don't give up. You never know what tomorrow may bring.

I wish nothing but the best for my parents, siblings, nieces and nephews. I hope that all of my family have peace and love in their lives, and that they have been able to break the cycle—whatever that may be—for themselves and their loved ones.

Nga mihi nui
Tim
(aka: My Timmy Me, the White Moko)

IMPORTANT PEOPLE

Aunty Mary Kapea, 2019

The matriarchs: Aunty Martha Hetaraka (left) and Aunty Nan (Hannah Cleaver), 2017

Roger at Mt Tabor, 1993

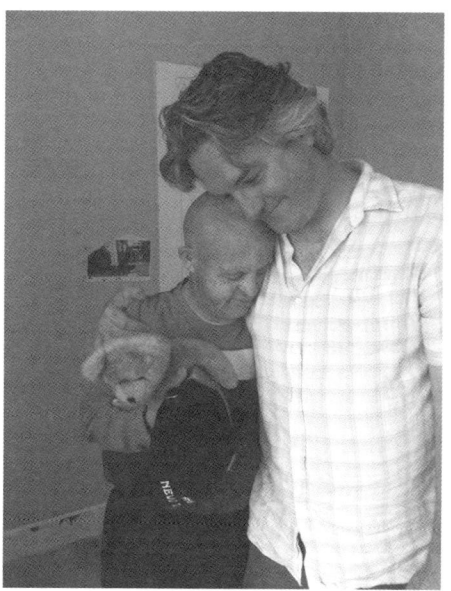
Roger at Mt Tabor, 2010

Childhood friend Vincent, 2019

Dr Masaaki Hatsumi, 34th Grandmaster of Togakure-ryu Ninjutsu and founder of Bujinkan Taijutsu. 5th Dan Black Belt, Tokyo, 2009

Finding love in Japan with a church group in Tokyo, 2009

Prof. Dave Millar
The induction into the
New Zealand Martial
Arts Hall of Fame, 2013

Ma and Ba's visit from China, 2018. In mandarin the term Ba is used, not Pa.

Nor-West News front page
after achieving a black belt, 1993

Teaching Warrior Kids, 1994

Ninja training, 1994

WARRIOR KIDS

Kura Toa
Warrior School
2012 - 2020

Kura Toa
Warrior School
2009 - 2012

Author visit at a school in
South Auckland, 2007

Henderson Warrior Kids and families, 1999

Warrior Kids workshop, 2007

Warrior Kids poster shoot, 2007

Starting circle, Warrior Kids, 2010

Time for sharing, Warrior Kids, 2010

FAMILY

Ping and baby,
Beijing 2006

Striving to be a good father,
2008

Back together in Beijing, 2017